The World Trade Center: The History Rebirth of a New Y

By Charles River Editors

Jeff Mock's picture of the Twin Towers and the rest of the World Trade Center

About Charles River Editors

Charles River Editors provides superior editing and original writing services across the digital publishing industry, with the expertise to create digital content for publishers across a vast range of subject matter. In addition to providing original digital content for third party publishers, we also republish civilization's greatest literary works, bringing them to new generations of readers via ebooks.

Sign up here to receive updates about free books as we publish them, and visit Our Kindle Author Page to browse today's free promotions and our most recently published Kindle titles.

Introduction

A picture of the Twin Towers and Battery Park

The Twin Towers

"The World Trade Center site will forever hold a special place in our city, in our hearts. " – New York City Mayor Michael Bloomberg

Before its destruction in the attacks on September 11, 2001, the World Trade Center in New York consisted of two of the world's most recognizable buildings, representing the strength and wealth of New York City in particular and the United States in general. That was the goal all along for philanthropist David Rockefeller, who had largely self-financed the development of One Chase Manhattan Plaza in the late 1950s in the hopes that the 70 story skyscraper would help spur further development nearby. Rockefeller envisioned Lower Manhattan as the site of a global financial center, full of stock exchanges, brokerages, investment banks, law firms, and other financial businesses.

The name "World Trade Center," when spoken by an American, tends to conjure up the best and worst about the nation. The idea for such a financial center was conceived of in the heady days of post-World War II prosperity, when the nation's financial prospects had never looked better and Americans were trading all over the world with both former allies and enemies. At the same time, many in New York City, one of the jewels of the East Coast, had fallen on hard times, and it was hoped that the World Trade Center would revitalize Lower Manhattan and bring the Big Apple a bigger share of the prosperity the world was enjoying. Likewise, the center was designed by men steeped in the modern era, when architects could build skyscrapers as opposed to simple office complexes.

As it would turn out, by the time construction on the buildings began, there were ominous clouds in the political and financial skies. The prosperity that had inspired its construction had given way to a financial malaise unlike any seen since the Great Depression, and many people were offended that money that could have gone to social programs was being used to build more office space. There was also political unrest, as many criticized the country's involvement in Vietnam. By the time the Twin Towers and the rest of the World Trade Center were completed, the project was considered by many to be not only a symbol of American prosperity but also another sign of capitalist greed.

For 30 years, the Twin Towers were the most dramatic features of the New York skyline, and for a short while one of the towers could boast of being the tallest building in the world. People came from around the world to visit them for both business and pleasure, and while most days were busy but uneventful, there were exceptions. A stunt seemingly featuring a man dancing in the sky humanized and popularized the buildings, and they began to prosper, just as the nation itself would rise again out of the mire of the 1970s. Almost as quickly, a fire threatened the North Tower in 1975. In 1977, a man decided to scale the side of the South Tower, and in 1983, a fireman completed a stunt designed to warn people about the impossibility of evacuating everyone in case of emergency.

Fatefully, the fireman's efforts fell on largely deaf ears, as no one could conceive of the need for such efforts. As everyone now knows, the World Trade Center could have stood for a century or more but didn't last half that long, because what they symbolically represented made them a physical target. The Twin Towers survived the first violent attack in 1993, but less than a decade later they were gone, the initial victims of a war still raging. The World Trade Center would be rebuilt, but New York City would never look the same again.

The World Trade Center: The History of the Construction, Destruction, and Rebirth of a New York City Landmark looks at the history of the original World Trade Center. Along with pictures of important people, places, and events, you will learn about the Twin Towers like never before.

The Freedom Tower

Bill Benzon's picture of the Freedom Tower

"I consider part of lower Manhattan to be hallowed ground. Nearly 3,000 people lost their lives in the World Trade Center towers... and for that reason alone, our nation should make absolutely sure that what gets built on 'Ground Zero' is an inspiring tribute to all who loved the Twin Towers, worked in them, and died there." – David Shuster

Since the earliest days of recorded human history, people have constructed buildings not just to provide shelter but to send a message. The earliest texts of Judaism speak of the patriarchs building to mark a place or event, while the Mayan leaders of South America built ziggurats not only to sacrifice their enemies but also to demonstrate their power to others. The Arc de Triomphe in France is just that, an arch to mark France's triumph over both its enemies and itself during the French Revolution and the Napoleonic Wars.

It should come as no surprise that in the dark days following the terrorist attacks of September 11, 2001, New York City began searching for some way to demonstrate its recovery and resolve. The obvious way to do just that was to rebuild what had been destroyed. Since there was no way to bring back the lives of those lost, the most straightforward path was to rebuild the Twin Towers that had fallen, but there was more to be done than to just rebuild the lost Twin Towers; the new building was to be bigger, taller, and better than before, as everyone hoped the country would somehow be.

In the decade that followed, the first of a new millennium, the Freedom Tower experienced many of the same ups and downs that the nation did. Plans to rebuild it were met with the same level of controversy as those to fight the war on terror. Likewise, its popularity ebbed and flowed with the fickle hearts of a people grown weary with fighting an enemy overseas and a poor economy at home. Political parties rose into and fell out of power, changing again and again the environment in which the builders were trying to work. At some points, it seemed that the project would never end.

Fortunately, the building itself finally knew victory and opened to the public, much as it seems the United States has made some inroads in the war against terror. At the same time, there is much left to do on both fronts, as the owners of One World Trade Center continue to try to rent out the space they have created, and those fighting terrorism at home and abroad continue to try to weed out the last vestiges of those who wish the nation ill. Ultimately, the final outcome on both fronts remains unknown, though much of the same spirit of patriotism and determination drives the leaders of the nation and the Center on to a much hoped for victory. Those who continue to wait wish them Godspeed, as they look on from a distance and close up at the flag flying at the top of the trade center and over the hills of Afghanistan.

The World Trade Center: The History of the Construction, Destruction, and Rebirth of a New York City Landmark looks at the construction history of the Twin Towers' replacement. Along with pictures of important people, places, and events, you will learn about the Freedom Tower like never before.

The World Trade Center: The History of the Construction, Destruction, and Rebirth of a New York City Landmark

About Charles River Editors

Introduction

   Chapter 1: Something Needs to Happen in Lower Manhattan

   Chapter 2: Office Space

   Chapter 3: Almost at the Limit of What Human Beings Can Create

   Chapter 4: A New Skyscraper Age or the Biggest Tombstones in the World

   Chapter 5: Staggering In Its Scale

   Chapter 6: A Big Civic Boondoggle

   Chapter 7: So Presumptuous, So Arrogant, So Naïve, So Romantic

   Chapter 8: Foreign Terrorists

   Chapter 9: There Will Be No Forgetting September the 11th

   Chapter 10: Considering a Replacement

   Chapter 11: Competition

   Chapter 12: Controversy

   Chapter 13: Cornerstone

   Chapter 15: Completion

   Chapter 16: Consummation

   Chapter 17: Consequence

Online Resources

Bibliography

Chapter 1: Something Needs to Happen in Lower Manhattan

"Ultimately the idea of a complex of buildings that they would call the World Trade Center got thrown out, because the port interests were still of such clout at that time that they were able to say, 'If you're going to spend money, you're going to build new piers.' But by the time David Rockefeller rises and replaces his uncle Winthrop Aldrich as the chief executive at Chase, it's a different place, New York, and the port is already on its way out. And something needs to happen in Lower Manhattan if it's going to regain the status that it once held as the world's financial center and that it was losing. ... I think that David Rockefeller was masterful in his introduction of the World Trade Center idea. And that idea was considered brilliant. He was called 'the billion dollar planner' by The New York Times. Mayor Wagner said it was wonderful. He, as all Rockefellers, knew how to build a power base and how to create momentum even before he released the idea to the public. And he did that. And so I think, although he only really proposed it, the fact that he proposed it really is why the World Trade Center was built." – Eric Lipton, *New York Times* reporter

In many ways, the concept of a "world trade center" was a completely 20th century notion for two reasons. The first is that, in all prior centuries, global trade was much more difficult without air shipping and instant communications systems like the telephone. People sailed around the world and traded items from one country to another, but there was no need for a central location; instead, trade was dispersed around the world with small offices set up in each trading area. On the other hand, it might be said that a world trade center, at least as it was conceived by its original builders, is no longer needed in the 21st century thanks to the Internet and e-commerce. On sites like Amazon and Ebay, people can buy and sell products from and to any nation on earth on a computer in their basements. Again, the power to trade is passing from the hands of a few central owners back into many small businesses.

As the Great Depression, which had plagued many countries, came to an end and World War II raged, the world suddenly felt smaller, and it seemed the idea of one place where buyers and sellers could meet together to do business was not just possible but desirable. In fact, the 1939 World's Fair featured a pavilion that bore the now famous name World Trade Center when it opened in Flushing, Queens, in 1939. One newspaper raved, "A headquarters for the national panel of arbitrators, of which five Chester businessmen are members, has been opened at the World Trade Center at the New York World's Fair, it was announced today by the American Arbitration Association. The members of the panel, which is made up of leading business men throughout the United States, act as lay judges in civil, commercial and intellectual disputes when parties to a controversy agree to settle their differences out of court. During their visit to the Center, the arbitrators will be provided with trade tours around the city and exposition. To help local visitors to understand the problems of commerce both here and abroad, introductions and contacts between foreign and domestic business men will be arranged. Available also will be the various facilities of the eight participating organizations of the World Trade Center, which include the use of a library and general information center on the commercial aspects of the Fair and City. To advise on local trade problems, the Department of Commerce has stationed at the Center a liaison officer expert in commercial relations. The facilities of the Center are also open to members of the Chamber of Commerce and their families. Courtesy cards may be obtained by writing to the Association in care of the World Trade Center at the World's Fair. Chester members of the arbitration tribunals who have been invited to participate in the activities of the World Trade Center, of which the American Arbitration Association Is a sponsoring member, include: Wallace Chadwick, A. B. Geary, Wallace Lippineou, R. C. Moleer and Raymond Munson."

Aerial photo of the 1939 Fair

While the names of the five men mentioned at the end of the article ultimately faded into history, their idea did not. Instead, it lay underground, slowly growing in the fertile financial ground of post-World War II America until, in the late 1950s, it sprang forward to blossom into reality.

At the time, the future of downtown New York was in question. Guy Tozzoli, who later became President of the World Trade Center Association, explained, "Lower Manhattan, which

I'll describe as the two square miles from Chambers Street down to the Battery, was dying. Companies were moving out, either to mid-Manhattan or really out of New York City. The only new building built since World War Two was the Chase Manhattan building. And David Rockefeller was then the chairman of the Chase Manhattan Bank. And so David had an idea. Why not create, using the Port Authority of New York and New Jersey, a 'world trade center' -- whatever that was."

David Rockefeller was heir to the famous Standard Oil Rockefeller family and a powerful New York real estate developer. In 1958, he teamed up with other similarly powerful business leaders to form the Downtown-Lower Manhattan Association (DLMA), telling the press, "Downtown Manhattan area is one of the most valuable and uniquely situated pieces of real estate in the entire world. The central core area of towering skyscrapers is surrounded by acres of marginal buildings the majority of which are more than a century old and only partly occupied." In November of that year, one small town editorial announced, "The most dramatic project for downtown development, perhaps, is the $1 billion program presented to New York City Oct 14 by the Downtown-Lower Manhattan Association, of which banker David Rockefeller is chairman of the executive committee."

David Rockefeller (left) and Eleanor Roosevelt circa 1953

Tozzoli

A few months later, another editorial, this one in the *New York Times*, added more details, with the most interesting part being about the location originally intended for the construction: "They are thinking large in downtown Manhattan. The World Trade Center, with a construction cost of perhaps a quarter of a billion dollars, proposed by the Downtown-Lower Manhattan Association, Inc, is the most important project for the economic future of the port of New York launched for many a year. As 'a headquarters to assure the expanding role of our country in international trade,' it has meaning that goes beyond dollars and goods, the encouragement of that friendly if competitive exchange of business with peoples throughout the world that makes for better understanding. We now begin to get the specifics of the billion-dollar redevelopment program first presented to Mayor Wagner in the fall of 1938 by the association led by David Rockefeller and John D. Butt. The clouds of uncertainty about the future downtown or waterfront areas had already been lifted as to lower Manhattan, which since 1950 has been enjoying a spectacular boom. In ten years thirty-five new major buildings have been completed or begun. The future of downtown Manhattan, already guaranteed by the confidence and leadership of its business men, now receives a further stimulant in the plan for the World Trade Center, several new buildings to be erected on a thirteen-acre site overlooking the East River south of Brooklyn Bridge…Rising from an elevated platform several blocks long, a World Trade Center Commerce Building of fifty to seventy floors with perhaps tens of these used as a hotel; a World Trade Mart, to be of low elevation in pleasing contrast, and finally a Central Securities Exchange Building to be erected if the Stock Exchange should elect to move are the fundamentals of this plan, now in preliminary schematic concept. A 3,500 ft - car parking garage would be built under the whole project. Shopping arcades and elevated plazas are interesting features. New York's prosperity, and that of the whole metropolitan area, depends to a degree not generally comprehended on the port area's unique position as a center of commerce — air, rail, over the road. The downtown Manhattan area is, of course, the historic focus of this tremendous business, this creator of employment and well-being. This new World Trade Center makes available the office space, the storage space, the exhibition space, the hotel and dining accommodations, the library and information resources, the convenience of proximity for all the varied elements that go into commerce and its promotion. For realization of the part of the plan appropriate to its chartered function the Port of New York Authority, qualified in every respect for the large undertaking, has been approached."

Making clear his enthusiasm for the project, the writer concluded, "To the courageous, intelligent leadership of the business men downtown responsible for such vision in planning, the people of New York and New Jersey owe grateful recognition. The World Trade Center is an exciting stimulating prospect."

Chapter 2: Office Space

"Nelson Rockefeller was a great and passionate builder. His greatest legacy was building stuff all over the place, in Albany and elsewhere. And he latched onto the Trade Center as a great project. It was felt that the Port Authority was the agency with the wherewithal to actually get it built, both because it had experience in building large and complicated projects, and because it had enormous bonding power and could finance this project without anything showing up on the state budget, so it made it a real win-win for Rockefeller. … There was a big fallacy, though, in this whole project. The real problem with Lower Manhattan was not that it didn't have enough office space. The problem was that it was hard to get to, particularly from the suburbs where a lot of business executives and bankers lived, and it was not a particularly appealing neighborhood in a general way, in that there were no places to eat, few places to shop, no cultural facilities to speak of, no places to live. All the things that make a neighborhood interesting and varied and meaningful as a part of the city, weren't there. And so the World Trade Center violated the first law of economics, really. It added to the supply of what there was already too much of, which was office space, without in fact doing anything to change the demand…But nobody quite got that." - Paul Goldberger, architecture critic

To accomplish their vision, the Downtown-Lower Manhattan Association hired architectural firm Skidmore, Owings and Merrill to create the design for the World Trade Center. The original plans proposed by Skidmore, Owings and Merrill included an exhibition hall, a 50-70 story tower and a new securities exchange building. At the time, the Downtown-Lower Manhattan Association hoped to entice the New York Stock Exchange to become the anchor tenant of the new development.

No project of such magnitude was going to be accomplished quickly, and Rockefeller and his partners had to wait for more than a year while the Port Authority studied the submitted plans. No matter what Rockefeller wanted, they would make the ultimate decision, a fact noted by architecture critic Paul Goldberger: "The Port Authority was run by Austin Tobin, who was a builder and planner who I think actually was better than Robert Moses at getting his will. He wasn't as famous as Moses because he operated a little more under the radar. Moses was too passionate about being in front of people and having fights with them, and therefore he lost from time to time. Tobin just very quietly, behind the scenes, manipulated and maneuvered and got things done, and got everything he ever wanted."

Tobin

Moses

Since the Port Authority was a joint venture between the State of New York and the State of New Jersey, the approval of both states was needed to build the World Trade Center. At first, New Jersey objected to the plan because the $300 million development would be built in New York, ostensibly leaving New Jersey with little benefit. After a new governor of New Jersey was elected, negotiations continued. While New Jersey's new administration was not completely opposed to the World Trade Center, as the previous administration was, it still opposed locating the World Trade Center on the East River rather than the Hudson River, which faces New Jersey. The Port Authority agreed to move the project to its current site near the Hudson River to placate New Jersey. Once New Jersey had signed on to the World Trade Center project, the plan moved forward. Tobin also wanted to change the name to the "World Trade Center" rather than describing it as a world trade center.

Needless to say, the fact that his older brother Nelson had recently been sworn in as the Governor of New York helped David Rockefeller's plan move more quickly through the vetting process. Still, in mid-February 1961, it wasn't a done deal, as the *Associated Press* reported, "The New Jersey Legislature is expected to approve tomorrow the final $470 million plan for the Port of New York Authority to reorganize the Hudson & Manhattan Railroad and build a world trade center in Manhattan. That was the word Saturday from Gov. Richard J. Hughes after a meeting between the staffs of Hughes and New York Gov. Nelson A. Rockefeller, which resulted in several amendments to the proposed legislation. Hughes said he believes that passage of the bill by New Jersey is assured. Rockefeller will present the measure to the New York Legislature soon. Bi-state approval is required for the projects. Hughes said New York agreed to addition of language in the bill to reassure that 'in no way' is the Port Authority empowered to build an air terminal. This meets Morris County fears that the legislation could open the door for the authority to go through with its much-opposed plan to build a jet airport in Morris County. At Saturday's session, a spokesman for Rockefeller said some changes proposed at a public hearing here were not accepted by Rockefeller's representatives."

The Port Authority finally signed off on the project on March 10, 1961. The Associated Press reported, "The Port of New York Authority has recommended that a huge world trade center be built in Lower Manhattan at a cost of $355 million. The center would include a 72- story world trade mart, a circular eight-story securities exchange, a 30-story world commerce exchange and a 20-story trade center gateway. The port authority…delivered its recommendation Saturday to Gov. Nelson A. Rockefeller of New York, Gov. Robert B. Meyner of New Jersey and Mayor Robert F. Wagner of New York."

Nelson Rockefeller

Meyner

By the end of the month, Tobin had created a new division in the Port Authority, the World Trade Office, and had appointed young Guy Tozzoli to run it, telling him, "You can pick the best of the Port Authority, because this is going to be our greatest project." Tozzoli later recalled, "I was given the job in February of 1962 to plan, to design, to construct, to operate the World Trade Center of New York. And there was only one thing, to achieve what David Rockefeller and Nelson Rockefeller wanted the Port Authority to do, I recommended to the board, you could only do one thing. You had to build what the Reader's Digest called 'the largest building project since the Egyptian pyramids.' There was no other way in this city, because this was the greatest city in the world. And it had to be something that people would pay attention to. Second thing we had to consider was, it had to be affordable.' So when they gave me the job, they said, 'By the way, it has to be self-supporting. So we're going to capitalize every paper clip that you use.' So I had hanging over me like the sword of Damocles, etc., 'You will make this thing work.'"

One of the first and most controversial moves Tozzoli made was to begin work on moving the site of the new center west toward the Hudson, which did not go over well with New York businessmen. However, the moved was deemed necessary if the new plan was to be accomplished in its full glory. Goldberger explained, "When the World Trade Center was conceived, the intention was not to build the world's tallest buildings. In fact, the preliminary designs on the east side were 60 or 70 stories. The first studies on the West Side were that. And then this sort of hubris, I think, took over and it just kept getting bigger and bigger, and they kept thinking they could do anything, and nobody said 'no.' I think the combination of David Rockefeller's passionate desire to put Lower Manhattan back on the map in a central way, in a really important way; the governor, his brother's, desire to just build bigger and bigger all the time anywhere; and the Port Authority's desire to really be the pre-eminent powerful civic authority in the world, let alone in New York -- all those things kind of combined to and as they sort of drifted to the West Side site from an original plan on the east side, it kind of drifted into being the world's tallest buildings."

Radio Row, one of the areas torn down to make room for the Twin Towers

With the plans in place, the Port Authority used its power of eminent domain to condemn over 150 buildings on the proposed site, which quickly brought lawsuits from business owners and land owners seeking to keep their property. These legal challenges lasted until 1963, but the Port Authority finally prevailed, clearing the way for the development of the plans. Finally, on November 13 of that year, an *Associated Press* article reported, "The Port of New York

Authority—backed by a U.S. Supreme Court decision—says it will move ahead immediately with the World Trade Center project on the Lower West Side of Manhattan. The announcement came shortly after the court refused Tuesday to rule on the constitutionality of a New York State law authorizing the project. Merchants whose businesses are on the project site have 25 days to apply for a rehearing of the suit they filed. The merchants argued that the law authorizing the center violates the U.S. Constitution by allowing the taking over of private property for non-public uses."

By 1964, the Port Authority began to lease space to commercial tenants and government entities.

Chapter 3: Almost at the Limit of What Human Beings Can Create

"To me it was a sense of building, creating something that's almost at the limit of what human beings can create, you know. I like that raw power. I like that sort of feeling that they were our Godzilla, you know, that they stood up there, that they say, 'So what?' you know, 'We are ugly -- so what.' You know? And they weren't, you know, because they were one thing one minute and they were another thing the other minute. You know, so you couldn't pass a judgment on them. You know those who would condemn them on an aesthetic basis, you know, were absolutely wrong, because it depended so much on how close you were, how far you were from them whether you saw them in the late afternoon, whether you saw them in the morning, whether you saw them in winter, whether you saw them in summer. So they were-- there was always a different feeling about them. I think, at some deeper level, there was the connection of the water to the sky. And I'm not very strong in mythology and all of this, but I think that played a very important role here--here you saw that somehow we're connected to something not just larger than New York, but larger than the earth itself." – Camilo Jose Vergara, photographer

By the time the Port Authority had cleared away the legal challenges, those in charge of the building project itself had decided that the new World Trade Center should be bigger and better than any other building in America. In explaining their mindset, Goldberger observed, "You know America has always believed in bigness. And I think we particularly believed in it in the 60s, when the World Trade Center was conceived. You know, bigger and bigger American things. Bigger and bigger doses of American power were going to solve anything. It was the age when all the cars were gargantuan and had fins. It was the age when we were sending troops into Vietnam. The age of going to the moon. Exactly. And its architectural equivalent was this notion of bigger and bigger buildings all the time. We've always also romanticized height in a very wonderful way, in New York. That's very much part of our DNA, is to just build bigger and taller all the time."

Of course, if an organization is going to take on such an ambitious project, it is critical to have the right people working on it. Otherwise, what should be a triumph can quickly become a fiasco. Tozzoli noted, "[The] first thing to do was to find the right architect. What I wanted, was a great architect. This had to be the greatest project in the world if it were to succeed. And we interviewed virtually everybody in the world, of consequence. And to the teams that I sent out to find out what architects did, the first stipulation I gave them was, 'Try to find somebody who you think is young enough to live for 20 years,' because I was sure that this project, as we conceived it, would take at least 20 years to finish. And it actually took more than that."

Already a bold man in charge of a bold project, Tozzoli made what initially seemed like yet another outlandish move by tapping Japanese-American architect Minoru Yamasaki in August 1962 to design the building. At that point, Yamasaki had never worked on a commercial project, nor had he ever designed the type of skyscraper that Tozzoli wanted. In describing his style in a 1959 interview, Yamasaki told a journalist, "Now our skylines are irregular but unstudied and consequently chaotic. Whereas if we studied our skylines we would be able to bring this sensation of aspiration and much more easily so because we have many different kinds of buildings which give us different kinds of silhouettes in our cities. ... And this, I think, can be so enhanced by architecture -- obviously you don't accomplish it all by architecture -- but nevertheless through architecture I think it becomes much easier if the architecture is thoughtful. And so consequently I feel that what we architects must think of is architecture as a result of human experience. And if we don't do this, then architecture becomes an abstract form, or a technique, or a clever device, or sculpture, of whatever it may be, which is only expressing your individual desire as an artist. Which is valid to a point. But nevertheless, since architecture is for all of us, and since we all participate in building it, I think that the role of the architect is somewhat more responsible than the individual artist and that he must think about the experience of people as he uses the building. In other words, if there are surprises, delight, or if he can gain a few fleeting moments of delight in some way, then this is a terribly important aspiration or delight, as I say, is a terribly important thing for us to accomplish in architecture. And I think this is possibly what we have been trying to do in our office."

Yamasaki

Yamasaki's first plan for the site included two Twin Towers, each 80 stories tall. Explaining his rationale for selecting a twin tower design, Minoru Yamasaki explained that "the obvious alternative, a group of several large buildings, would have looked like a housing project." However, Yamasaki's 80 story towers did not satisfy the Port Authority, which required that the site have at least 10 million square feet of office space. When Yamasaki was told that his design must include 10 million square feet of rentable office space, he later admitted that he believed the requirement "was a terrifying program from the standpoint of size. You just run scared before you get adjusted."

The Port Authority's requirement induced Yamasaki to alter his design by increasing the height of the towers to 110 stories each. Tozzoli recalled, "He must have done 50 or more different models, limited by the 16-acre site that we had. And finally he sent word back to me, 'It's time for you to come out and I want to show you the one I like the best.' He had done Twin Towers and a plaza about the size of Piazza San Marco, just a little smaller than that. And it had a hotel, and it had the Customs House, everything around it. It was a lovely, lovely design. And so I said to Yama when I saw it, I said, 'This is very fine design.' But 'Does it meet my program?' 'No,' he said. 'It's two million feet short.' I said, 'Why is that?' Well, he said, 'The towers are 80 floors high.' Said, 'You can't build a building taller than 80 floors.' I said, 'Why not?' Well, he said, 'Because the configuration, the elevators take too much space. That's why no one has ever done that.' And I remember saying to him, 'You know, Yama, President Kennedy is going to put a man on the moon. You're going to figure out a way for me to build the world's tallest buildings, because that'll get us the other two million feet of space. We'll just make those towers higher.'"

Leslie Robertson, the engineer who would be tasked with making Yamasaki's vision a reality, later admitted, "I'm sure Guy Tozzoli said, '90's not high enough; a hundred's not high enough; 'how about more space?' And I think he may not admit it but my guess is he was cognizant of the fact that the Trade Center was going to become a real image of New York City. And he had high aspirations that that be the case."

One of the major challenges of the 110 story high towers was elevator design. Each elevator shaft takes a portion of every floor, so the number of traditional elevators required would eat up an enormous portion of the floor space in a 110 story tower. To get around this problem, Yamasaki's design included both express as well as traditional elevators, a system based on New York City's subway system, which has express trains that only stop at certain stops in conjunction with local trains that stop at every stop.

Although they no longer had any legal issues blocking their progress, those striving to build the towers still faced an uphill battle, including opposition from many who felt that the Port Authority should stick to matters concerning the port and leave inland issues to others. As writer Pete Hamill put it, "This is not the business of the Port Authority. The Port Authority should be talking about the port. If we're losing the ocean liners, what are we going to put there?"

Chapter 4: A New Skyscraper Age or the Biggest Tombstones in the World

"The Port Authority was never founded to go into the real estate business, but it's the most profitable business in New York. And they saw great profits and ways of supporting their projects, which up to a certain point you could understand, although I think they should have not gone into the real estate business to begin with. ... Well, that was the urban renewal formula of the '60's, that was so disastrous in cities across the country: the idea of clearing out, supposedly getting rid of blight, which unfortunately was a synonym for history, and for small business. And then to substitute these superblocks with huge buildings. The real estate community had an expression -- ripe for redevelopment. You cut off, you closed, or there's an official word for that, too, you de-mapped, wonderful old streets and small buildings that gave you the history and the flavor and the continuity of the city, and you put them together for a superblock. For the World Trade Center, 14 historic streets became two superblocks. ... Who's afraid of the big, bad buildings? Everyone, because there are so many things about gigantism that we just don't know.

The gamble of triumph or tragedy at this scale -- and ultimately it is a gamble -- demands an extraordinary payoff. The Trade Center towers could be the start of a new skyscraper age or the biggest tombstones in the world." – Ada Huxtable, architecture critic

In January 1964. Yamasaki's modified design was released to the public. The design called for the buildings to have metal facades, which led to mixed reviews from architecture critics. Some panned the design as unimaginative, with one critic calling the buildings "nothing more than glass and metal filing cabinets." Other critics complained that the Twin Towers would ruin New York City's iconic skyline, potentially disrupt radio and television reception in parts of the city, and strain the city's services. Nonetheless, one editorial at the time captured the appeal of the Twin Towers: "New York City had many black marks against it but it is also a city of unrivaled progress. Large in area, huge in population, it builds in keeping with its size. The weekend's unveiling of the model for the New York Port Authority's World Trade Center reflects the spirit of the city. This structure is to tower 110 stories into the air, 100 feet higher than the Empire State building without its television mast. But the trade center is not to be one tower 1,350 feet tall but two might pillars of metal and glass. They will be fit companions of the new Narrows Bridge now under construction and also the largest of its kind in the world. It is not difficult to predict that the World Trade Center will not be universally acclaimed. Some will call it a monstrosity but somehow we doubt this. ... Safety experts may claim that the towers will be a danger to air traffic and bird lovers will declare them a death trap to migratory birds. They may ask why it is necessary to keep thrusting higher and higher into the sky. The real estate and tax experts could offer reasons but the real one must be that men have always sought heights. Heights makes some people feel superior to those below: other to feel nearer to God."

From the moment the plans were released, some people were concerned about the impact that 10 million square feet of office space would have on the New York City real estate market, and among those most concerned were the owners of New York's most famous skyscraper. According to Tozzoli, "The main objection to this project came from the people who owned the Empire State Building. The Empire State Building was owned by Harry Helmsley and Larry Wien. And they, when they heard the announcement of our plan, which was in 1964, they formed a 'Committee for a Reasonable World Trade Center.' And they gave them a budget of $500,000 to prevent the construction of the World Trade Center. So I went and met with Mr. Helmsley one day. I said, 'Harry' -- I knew him -- I said, 'Harry, could you tell me what is a reasonable World Trade Center?' And he said, 'Yes.' I said, 'What's that?' He said, '100 floors high.' And I said, 'Well, your Empire State Building's 102.' And I said, 'I'm sorry, but I think 110 is a better number.' ... My mother, who loved television she said, 'You know, you're my son and I love you very much, but I must tell you, if you're going to hurt television reception in this area, you better stop that project of yours right now.' And I knew I had big problems. In any case, we did. We actually negotiated a deal with the television people, and they moved down to our place. And it all worked out."

Opposition came from a number of places, but it came primarily from those who were concerned about the impact the buildings would have on Lower Manhattan. Naturally, many hated the idea of losing the past to make way for the future. Architect Robert Stern explained, "The Trade Center was being realized at a time when there was what could be described as a paradigm shift about architecture and urban development. Preservation was a growing sentiment among a wide number of people in New York and other places at this time. Remember the Pennsylvania Station protest was '63, the destruction '66. It's just those years the Trade Center is being hatched and developed. And so you have these two models of urbanism or urban growth coming head to head at the Trade Center site. So people were very much divided as to whether this project should even happen." Stern admitted he was in the camp of critics: "I started out not liking the World Trade Center, because the World Trade Center was the Conrad Veidt of buildings. Conrad Veight was 'the man you loved to hate.' The World Trade Center were the buildings you loved to hate. I was very much around when the process of the clearing of the site and the protests about the destruction of that kind of funky agglomeration of street patterns and activities around it were there. I resented its massive dumbness, its huge size -- the fact that it tipped the balance of the skyline to the west in an unnatural way -- if you can call something like a manmade skyline of Manhattan natural."

For others, it wasn't just the loss of buildings but the end of a way of life. New York had been built by immigrant families who opened up small businesses throughout the city, and many of them stood to be driven out. Writer Pete Hamill remembered, "I really felt the assault on Cortlandt Street, because you slowly began to look at the plans as they emerge, and you find out there's not going to be a Cortlandt Street. They're going to have a sign that says Cortlandt Street, and after that it will be nothing but concrete and a plaza into which nobody ever stepped."

Obviously, those who were in favor of building the new towers had a different perspective, as Stern noted: "If you're a planner, you look at the map; or you're in an airplane, you look down at the city, you see this area: four-story buildings, slightly tumbled down in appearance; what would appear to be marginal retail uses -- electronics shops and so forth. So in the mentality of post-World War Two redevelopment, this was a soft area, an easy kill: hardly anybody to relocate; no institutions to relocate; and nobody living there, to speak of. So there it was, quick: one-two-three, do it. But by the time the site began to be really getting ready for clearance, people saying, 'You're tearing out this living, vital part of the city.'"

Before long, those opposing the new building plans literally took their fight to the streets, protesting and insisting that they would stop the project. Their leader, Oscar Nadel, demanded, "Now, for the last time I might say with respect to the Port Authority: stay out of private enterprise you were told to build bridges and tunnels. And airports, build them. Stay in your business and we'll stay in ours." Of course, that did not happen, and Tobin tried to offer a somewhat empathetic response: "We're talking here about things in the public interest in a free country that concern not a few store owners on a block down in this area, but we're concerning something that's not tens of thousands or hundreds of thousands, but millions of people and their livelihoods in this area and the whole future of this area in its great port which is the foundation of its welfare in the future. And those are the issues here and not any phony issue of the Port Authority wanting to get into the real estate business, which is the last thing in the world it has the slightest interest in."

Chapter 5: Staggering In Its Scale

"In city after city great new office buildings, cubes of glass and steel, go up. Yet badly needed schools are not built, and with a revolt against proliferating taxes at every level of government, bond issues for schools and other public needs are repeatedly voted down. The justification for the office buildings is that they go on the tax rolls and provide badly needed public revenue. Because it is being built by the Port of New York Authority, the World Trade Center itself will not be subject to taxation. It is being financed by tax-exempt bonds issued by the Authority. All office, store and hotel space leased to private enterprise will be taxable. And the Authority is paying the city money in lieu of taxes — $6,125,000 the first year, which covers the taxes paid on buildings torn down to make way for the center. The Center is staggering in its scale. The mind reels with statistics. Forty thousand door knobs. Air-conditioning sufficient to cool 15,000 homes. Rentable space of 230 acres, more than in the 18 buildings in Rockefeller Center. The electricity consumed will equal that of a city the size of Schenectady, N.Y. A goal is to restore downtown Manhattan and at the same time help buttress New York's port against growing competition. ... The will is there to restore downtown Manhattan. Thus far the will has been in woefully short supply to restore Harlem and the other Manhattan of the festering slums." - Marquis Childs, Letter to the Editor, June 29, 1969

Despite the protests, on March 21, 1964, workers took the first step toward building the new World Trade Center by tearing down old buildings in the area. This was brutal for many of those watching, including Hamill: "I remember seeing Cortlandt Street being shoveled off to become landfill for what became Battery Park City. I mean, literally, bulldozers knocked down the old houses and just tipped them over, smashed them over like they were big fists being leveled from the sky somehow. Among the many things that were lost on September 11th were the final Polaroid photographs of the houses on Cortlandt Street with their prices that were labeled on them by the assessors, what the owners were going to get paid, you know, $9,000, $12,000, $18,000, whatever it was. All those original Polaroids, no negatives, were lost in one of the buildings on September 11th, so that even that, even that record of it is gone."

Less than half a year later, on August 5, workers were able to begin rebuilding over the areas they had torn down, excavating the deep hole that would form the foundation for the new buildings. This was a problem, since the ground they were digging into was mostly waterlogged landfill first constructed by early English settlers. As they dug out a hole that many referred to as a bathtub (because of the way it filled with water), they found everything from cannonballs to English coins to ship-anchors. Later, they constructed "slurry walls" that used concrete poured into metal cages to drive out the water.

Unfortunately, the foundations laid by the workers were just the beginning of the challenges they faced. Robertson later observed, "The Trade Center had a different kind of structure. It was built more like the wing of an airplane. In the wing of the airplane, the strength is all in the surface of the wing, or the fuselage, in both cases. All of the interior columns that had been used in the past were a detriment. They were harmful to the design, because we didn't want those interior columns. We wanted that weight out on the outside, where it would do some good for the stalwartness of the building in resisting these giant loads from the wind. ... And so we had to rethink the entire process. How much can a building move in the wind? How much would they oscillate? No one had ever found out. No one had ever tried to find out, even, or even thought there was an issue to find out about. Not only how much does it move; how much can it move?"

To solve this problem, Robertson came up with the unique solution of putting specialized sorts of shock absorbers in the building. They would ultimately allow any swaying caused by the wind to bleed off harmlessly into the ground below. According to Tozolli, the completed towers "could resist a 150-mile wind blowing consecutively on one side of the building for 30 minutes, and they would not fall down. I used to say they move like a snake. Different from all other buildings in the world, the strength to resist the wind is in the outside walls instead of the elevator core, which is normal for all other highrise buildings in the world. And so these towers were much stronger, if you would."

Another unique feature of the towers was that they were not built on site, piece by piece, but instead constructed of prefabricated sections, each three stories tall and each constructed off site. This allowed the construction process to move along at enviable speed. Robertson explained, "We had experimented with pre-prefabrication in a few buildings, but never even close to the scale that it was done on the World Trade Center. Huge prefabricated elements, constructed all over the United States, with materials that came from all over the world, and finally assembled into one building in New York City. We had steelwork being fabricated in Los Angeles, in Dallas, in Seattle, in Pittsburgh, in Virginia, and down into Georgia and up into Canada. And all of that was coordinated through our offices."

Once the pieces arrived, they were quickly put in place as the next sections of the massive puzzle Tozzoli was putting together. 3,600 men worked every day to place 800 tons of steel, and the massive pieces were raised into the sky by four giant cranes. Tozzoli praised the crew, saying, "The Koch Erecting Set were the incredible people who ran the job. And I still see Mr. Koch from time to time and I remind him, not one ironworker was killed in the construction of the World Trade Center. And this is what they used to do. They'd be up on the steel, and they'd look out, and they'd say, 'We're going to be all right today, boys. Mr. Koch just went to mass.' There's a little Catholic church down there. He went at eight o'clock every morning. And they said, 'That takes care of us for the day.' And sure enough, not a single ironworker died. Now of course, the building lent itself to that because we put steel up on the outside walls. And then you could only fall two or three floors, if you ever fell off. But that was the way it was."

In spite of the speed with which the men were working, Robertson made sure that everything was done with the highest standards of safety in mind. In fact, he considered the future safety of the building and all who worked in it his personal responsibility, later recalling with more than a little sense of irony, "One of my jobs was to look at all of the possible events that might take place in a highrise building. And of course there had been in New York two incidences of aircraft impact, the most famous one of course being on the Empire State Building. Now, we were looking at an aircraft not unlike the Mitchell bomber that ran into the Empire State Building. We were looking at aircraft that was lost in the fog, trying to land. It was a low-flying, slow-flying 707, which was the largest aircraft of its time. And so we made calculations, not anywhere near the level of sophistication that we could today. But inside of our ability, we made calculations of what happened when the airplane goes in and it takes out a huge section of the outside wall of the building. And we concluded that it would stand. It would suffer but it would stand. And the outside wall would have a big hole in it, and the building would be in place. What we didn't look at is what happens to all that fuel. And perhaps we could be faulted for that, for not doing so. But for whatever reason we didn't look at that question of what would happen to the fuel."

A picture of the World Trade Center under construction in 1969

A picture of water being drained from the construction site

Chapter 6: A Big Civic Boondoggle

"The impact of the Trade Center on the Lower Manhattan environment was really rather devastating. The plaza in front of the World Trade Center was a concrete football field. It was not an appealing place at all. Most of the shopping and activity took place underground, which was at a further remove from the street life of New York. The buildings only succeeded as abstract objects. They did succeed ultimately pretty well as abstract objects, but it is not out of abstract geometric forms that you make a city. You make a city out of street life. And the World

Trade Center pushed away the street life of Lower Manhattan in favor of something very different. ... At the beginning, because there was not nearly enough business to fill it, it was bailed out by its builders. Governor Nelson Rockefeller committed to putting offices of the State of New York into one tower, and the Port Authority moved all of its own offices into the other. So in fact, it was mostly a big civic boondoggle, in effect, and had only a minimal amount of tenants who were actually part of the original concept." - Paul Goldberger

During the years it took to build the World Trade Center, the very nature of American society shifted in ways that no architect or engineer could foresee. In time, the optimism of the early 1960s gave way to a growing sense of unrest and despair over the national economy, race relations, and the Vietnam War. Stern admitted, "The Trade Center's finished at a time when the economy is in the toilet -- I think that's the best way to put it. The Vietnam War has ripped the country apart. The divisiveness of the young versus the old, the 'haves' versus the 'have nots,' had never been greater than perhaps except in the case of the Civil War. And there were these two monsters, huge, undifferentiated buildings, rising here, and the context around them hadn't even been finished."

A picture of the construction in 1970 by Pat Bianculli.

Many people succumbed to despair during this difficult time and, unfortunately for the project, one of them was Austin Tobin. As he fought with the governor of New Jersey on one side and the mass transit authorities on the other, he lost a crucial ally: the New York press. One reason for the latter was that the American press became very anti-business in the early '70s, but another reason is that many people just didn't like change. Goldberger explained, "I remember being offended that the title for the tallest building was being taken away from the Empire State Building, a building that I liked much more and felt represented the spirit of New York much better than the World Trade Center. And I remember thinking, you know, this whole thing is a sort of gargantuan piece of banality."

In fact, by the time the North Tower was completed in December 23, 1970, the American people had largely lost interest in the project. Tozzoli recalled, "December 1970. The reason I remember it is the last piece of steel went up and the next day the first tenant moved into the bottom of the building. Actually two tenants moved in that day, and on the ninth and 10th floors." The South Tower was completed seven months later, on July 19, 1971.

When all was said and done, the Twin Towers contained nearly 200,000 tons of steel, and each stood 1,360 feet tall, but at first it seemed people hardly noticed. Photographer Camilo Jose Vergara recalled, "There was some sense that there was something insane here that was -- that was being done, because there was no need for it. This was a city that was getting into more and more trouble, where the city finances were terrible, where crime was rising, where all of the problems that then came to a head in '75, where the almost bankruptcy of the city, were all there. And yet they were putting this building up! And you'd say, 'What's going on?'"

In fact, it often seemed that those who were ignoring the towers were the merciful ones, because the project fell under increasing criticism, even among the tenants. Stern conceded, "Of course people hated, you know, working in the Trade Center. The reason it was filled up was because the space was cheaper than a comparable space in lower buildings. They hated it because the elevator systems [were a] nuisance to go up and down. It was like you planned whether you had to actually leave your office because it was so inconvenient. I think the Trade Center was also a terrible failure on an urban design level or a public space level. The plaza was dead. The plaza managed to be dead, not only in day-to-day use, or even for the occasional festival, but could never quite fill it. But even in the movies, when they made *The Wiz* or when they made the second version of *King Kong*, it still couldn't come to life. It just resisted vitality."

Such was the universal dislike of the towers that the project even became a subject of study by business students who were being taught what not to do. A 1971 *United Press International* story reporting on a business course noted, "A practical example of the problems studied in the program is an analysis of the history and prospects of the vast new World Trade Center being completed in lower Manhattan. In a course entitled Interorganizational Decision Making given [by] Dr. Arie Y. Lewin, the students came up with a report criticizing the Port of New York Authority and the city for failing to give enough consideration to the long range need of transporting an additional 60,000 persons daily in and out of the vicinity of the trade center."

In fact, one of the problems that surprised the Port Authority most was how difficult it was to interest people in moving into the buildings. Within just a few years of opening, the World Trade Center was losing an average of $1 million a month, and when it rained during the dedication ceremony on April 4, 1973, many must have bitterly thought it was symbolic. The ceremony got little press, with most papers only showing a picture of the towers and a caption similar to this one: "With its Twin Towers soaring 1,350 feet above Manhattan, the World Trade Center officially became the world's tallest building at dedication ceremonies Wednesday. But the honor will be short-lived, since an even taller building is under construction in Chicago. When completed, Chicago's Sears Tower will rise to 1,450 feet. The Trade Center, which took seven years to build, has been partially occupied since 1970 and will not be fully completed until next year. Eventually some 50,000 persons will be doing business there."

Peter Brennan, the U.S. Secretary of Labor, was supposed to be the guest of honor but never made it there, and New York Mayor John Lindsay also failed to show. Even Tobin refused to attend, claiming that the weather kept him away. Tozzoli later recalled, "You know, we named the plaza the Austin Tobin Plaza, long after he left. And Austin, we knew, was very sick. And I think of all the projects that the Port Authority did, I think Austin felt that the Trade Center was his greatest. And I got a call one day, and he came down in a wheelchair. And I wheeled him out to the plaza. And he asked if he could be left alone. And Austin sat in that wheelchair for almost two hours. And he looked at the plaza and the great sculpture that was in the plaza, and he could see the hotel and the Customs House and the commodity building and the Nagare sculpture's beautiful, and Fritz Koenig's sculpture, which was in the middle of that fountain. Those were great works of art. And I remember leaving him there, and then I came and got him. And I never saw him again after that. He died almost within weeks after that one moment, two hours, being out there looking at the plaza of the World Trade Center, named after him."

Brennan

Lindsay

Pictures of the sphere and the Tobin Plaza

Chapter 7: So Presumptuous, So Arrogant, So Naïve, So Romantic

"I was in a dentist's waiting room in Paris with a giant toothache, and I was looking at what usually, you know, look through those old magazine, old newspapers. And somehow I fell onto a small article, but the picture really called my attention. It was the Twin Towers but in their model form, because it was in 1968 and they had not yet started to be built. And I had not yet started to be a wire walker, which is actually the amazing part of the story. So how could I fall in love with those two towers, the highest towers in the world, said the article? So presumptuous, so arrogant, so naive, so romantic. And it was all of that. And I remember, I just -- I had to tear the article, and everybody was watching me. You know, in France everybody's watching each other. It was very quiet, and I couldn't rip the page, and plus you don't, you know, you don't steal something. So I actually let go a giant sneeze and under the cover of the sneeze, I teared the article, put it under my shirt, and I had to leave, and I had to find another dentist. But you know, what was it to have a toothache for another week, when what I had now in my chest was a dream?" - Philippe Petit

As the Twin Towers were being completed, some people dreamed of working in them, and plenty of people dreamed of visiting them and riding the elevator to the top of the observation area, but one man wanted more; he wanted to walk on the very air between them. 24 year old Philippe Petit flew from his home in France to New York City in January 1974 in search of his ultimate dream, later explaining, "When I came to New York, it was winter. And I had a little journal or a little whatever, I wrote my thoughts. And I thought: It's old, it's dirty, it's full of skyscrapers, I love it. That was my first little entry the first day I saw New York. I remember my first encounter with the Twin Towers. I got out of the subway -- it was a long subway ride -- and out of the darkness I emerged at the base of one of the tower, and look up. And like a slap in the face I saw that my dream was impossible. I mean, it was right there in aluminum and glass and steel and concrete behind it. It was right there. It said: impossible. And yet somehow I actually find myself trespassing over the plaza, still under construction, and sneaking in one of the tower and climbing and climbing inside the building, until I find myself very close to the top, and until there were no more windows, no more partitions. There were just the skeleton, the beautiful steel columns and beams of the building. And then I emerge and there were no gates. There were nothing to protect you from the devouring void. And I stand and I looked. And the second I look at the other tower, another time the word impossible etch itself inside me. But somehow I went back down and looked again from the street, and there I realize, it's impossible. But I'll do it."

A picture of Philippe Petit by Chrisa Hickey.

Once he had made up his mind, there was nothing for Petit to do but plan how to make his dream a reality. He continued, "And there was the beginning of a second wave of work -- the real work, the work of getting into the building, not into archaeological findings or architectural magazines, but this time it was the monster, the beast, getting into the belly of the beast every day, which I did, hiding myself, disguising myself, sneaking, being caught, abandoning the project, going back to it, for eight months -- eight months in New York. And the towers, the more I got to know them, the more they become an ally. That's why, when I say I conquered them, probably it's wrong. I married them, certainly. But they became my friends."

One of the first things Petit did was to snag an interview with Tozzoli and a private tour of the Twin Towers. According to Tozzoli, "later on, I recognized that the subject always got back to how those towers move in the wind." Obviously, Petit needed to know how the wind would affect his stunt, and after studying and planning, he returned to the buildings in the early evening of August 6, 1974. One team in each building made their way to the top to help him achieve his dream.

When Petit and the teams arrived at the top, they quickly encountered some obstacles. The tight rope walker explained, "The first problem was how to pass the cable across, how to pass the first line, which will ultimately become a rope strong enough to pull a heavy steel cable. So how to get that fishing line across? It's like 200 feet from center of roof to center of roof, roughly. We had all kind of ideas. And the idea that prevailed was the one I thought was ridiculous, was a bow and arrow. But it actually worked. So with a fishing line and a bow and arrow we passed the first line across. And then all night we pulled, and then the cable was secured."

The men worked through the night under the cover of darkness to string a one inch cable across the 130 foot wide expanse between the two buildings, and the next morning, just after 7:00 a.m., Petit took his first step off the towers and into history. At first, no one seemed to notice what was going on just above their heads, but as people started to look up and see the unbelievable sight, they pointed it out to others nearby. Before long a crowd had gathered, staring with their mouths agape at the man on the wire, and they got the performance of a lifetime. Petit described the stunt: "Somehow I found myself spending 45 minutes and doing eight crossings. There were thousands of people, at some point a hundred thousand people. And actually, at some point during these different crossings, I actually could hear my audience a quarter of a mile below. And I could hear them punctuating what I was doing on the wire. Let's say if I would take a bow on one leg, or salute the horizon, or kneel in front of a tower to say hello to the tower, I would hear, almost with an echo, the people cheering, screaming, applauding."

Like many people in New York that morning, Tozzoli was just trying to get to work through the traffic when he heard something that initially astonished and then concerned him: "I had in my car a radio that connected me to the police desk at the World Trade Center. And on the day in question the light went on. And the patrolman at the police desk said, 'Mr. T, there's a problem in the World Trade Center.' I said, 'What's the problem?' He said, 'There's a guy walking on a tightrope between the two towers. What should we do?' And I couldn't think of anything else. I said, 'Don't let him fall off,' and I hung up. So then I drove a little further. I called back. I said, 'By the way, this is incredible. There's somebody walk--If he doesn't fall off, and he comes off, don't arrest him.'"

Charles Daniels, a sergeant with the Port Authority Police, was one of the first to arrive at the scene that morning. For a while, he stood transfixed by the most elegant crime he had ever seen. "Well, after arriving on the rooftop Officer Meyers and I observed the tightrope 'dancer' because you couldn't call him a 'walker' approximately halfway between the two towers. And upon seeing us he started to smile and laugh and he started going into a dancing routine on the high wire. He then went down to one knee and we stepped to the background and I said for everyone to be quiet. And at this time he laid down on the high wire and you know, just lackadaisically rolled around on the wire like. He got up he started walking and laughing and dancing. And he turned around and ran back out into the middle. He was bouncing up and down. His feet were actually leaving the wire and then he would resettle back on the wire again. Unbelievably really. To the point that we just everybody was spellbound in the watching of it. And I personally figured I was watching something that somebody else would never see again in the world. Thought it was once in a lifetime."

Once the police arrived, Petit's show was over; the next time he got to one of the towers, he was arrested and hauled down the elevator to the police station located in the basement of the South Tower. The officers charged him with 14 different crimes, all of them misdemeanors, before releasing him.

Not surprisingly, reporters were waiting for him, and the following exchange capped off the day:

> "Reporter: Why did you do this?
>
> Petit: That's the thousandth 'why' this morning. There's no why. Just because when I see a beautiful place to put my wire, I cannot resist.
>
> Reporter: Weren't you afraid up there at all?
>
> Petit: I was not afraid. But I was just looking what I had in front of me. I have really something which was huge and incredible, you know. So afraid, not, but living more than a thousand percent. So perhaps that's close to afraid, I don't know. But at the same time I was happy, happy, happy, happy."

The walk proved to be not just a watershed moment for Petit but the World Trade Center as well by bringing the Twin Towers some much-needed positive attention. In gratitude for what the young man had done, Tozzoli interceded with the police to have the charges against him dropped. He later explained, "It's just that this guy had done this, and it made the towers belong, if you would, more to New York."

For its part, the Port Authority, which had first arrested him, subsequently granted him a free pass for life to the observation deck.

After Petit's stunt, the buildings became a challenge of sorts to those who craved extra adventure. A few years later, in 1977, George Willig decided to try something no one had before. On May 27, a *United Press International* story reported, "'It was a lot of fun,' Willig, 27, said Thursday as he met reporters after being booked for trespassing, reckless endangerment and disorderly conduct. His alleged crime — mounting the 110-story World Trade Center with only a homemade climbing device and his determination not to be denied his conquest. 'The only time I was scared was when I started, because I was afraid I'd get caught before I got going,' he said. With his arms and legs splayed against the sheer face of the 1,350-foot building, Willig made the ascent in about 3 1/2 hours along the window washing tracks cut into the northeast corner of the south tower. When he cleared the parapet and was hauled atop the roof at 10:04 a.m., thousands of rubbernecks below, many of whom had watched the entire climb, let out a thunderous cheer heard throughout lower Manhattan. A quarter mile above them, the 5 foot-11, 155-pound Willig, wearing a blue bandana and a multicolored, striped shirt, waved blistered hands at his admirers who clogged the streets below. Horns blew. 'He's up there! He's on top and he's safe!' one man shouted in the street. Life in the nation's largest city returned to normal."

Chapter 8: Foreign Terrorists

"America's sense of immunity from foreign terrorists was shattered Feb. 26 when a home-made bomb exploded two floors beneath the World Trade Center, killing six and injuring 1,000. The case was cracked when a suspect tried to reclaim the $400 deposit on a rented van used to transport the bomb. Sheik Omar Abdel-Rahman and a band of Muslim followers were charged in the plot. The FBI thwarted terrorist attempts to bomb other New York City landmarks and symbols of capitalism." - *Associated Press*, December 31, 1993

A picture of the South Tower lobby interior by Raphael Concorde

When the observation deck atop the South Tower opened in 1975, the World Trade Center went from being exclusively a business complex to becoming one of the most popular tourist destinations in New York. A year later, the Towers stood like proud parents at a birthday party as New York harbor became clogged with boats and ships gathered to celebrate the nation's bicentennial. However, it was the opening of the rooftop restaurant some months later that led food critic Gael Greene to gush, "Suddenly I knew that New York would survive. If money and power and ego could create this extraordinary pleasure and instant landmark, money and power and ego could rescue the city from its ashes."

A picture of the Windows on the World restaurant by Raphael Concorde

Was money and power and ego enough? Maybe for the wealthy and powerful and egotistical. But the common people, the men and women whose tax dollars would go to pay for much of what it took to build and maintain the World Trade Center, needed more. Fortunately, they found it with these attractions. Tozzoli opined, "The observation deck and Windows on the World were the two things, in my judgment, that turned the city of New York from looking at the Trade Center as some monster downtown to something that was theirs. They began to adopt it. And it was great. It was so successful that you had to wait seven months to get a Saturday night reservation there, unless you knew somebody. It was incredible. And we were consistently the highest grossing restaurant in the whole world."

A picture of sightseers on the observation deck by Ted Quackenbush

In a rather short amount of time, native New Yorkers came to view the Twin Towers as symbols of pride and prosperity, and for people coming into the city, it was impossible not to notice them. In movies, the Twin Towers symbolized New York much the same way the Empire State Building did, and their presence or absence would become a way to mark time in photographs of the skyline. Stern noted, "These kinds of things give a building a human dimension. One would hope that the building would have a human dimension in its design. That has always been debatable, with the case of the Trade Center. But events did happen that showed that this could be brought into the city and into the life of the city. Another thing about the Trade Center that changed it was the whole changing character of Lower Manhattan. People began to live downtown. And they rather liked the Trade Center, the big open space. And then the people living in Tribeca -- also the people living in Battery Park City began to see these buildings as an identifiable landmark in their neighborhoods, in their daily lives. You know, you could orient yourself. You knew where you were in relationship to the Trade Center towers."

By the end of the 1980s, the buildings were running at full capacity. Among the 110 stories in each tower, 8 were occupied by building services, including mechanical rooms for the elevators, but all of the other floors were rented out. The first tenants were governmental entities, including the State of New York and the Port Authority itself, but, as Rockefeller had hoped, large financial institutions were attracted by the high profile buildings and the open floor plans. Morgan Stanley eventually moved into the towers, as did other investment banks, including Salomon Brothers and Cantor Fitzgerald. Aon Corporation, a large insurer, also became a tenant. Each of the towers contained a massive 3.8 million square feet of office space. 50,000 people worked in the Twin Towers, and another 200,000 people visited each day. Indeed, the buildings were like a city unto themselves, with their own post offices, shops, restaurants, a train station, and even their own zip code.

As the 1990s dawned, the once white elephants had become shining examples of American power. As Tozzoli satisfactorily put it, "It turned out fine. The Trade Center was self-supporting. In fact, when I retired from the Port Authority of New York in 1987, the World Trade Center of New York was making more than $133 million a year, net, net, net. So, you know, it worked. And then all those buildings in Lower Manhattan, all the jobs that it created for people."

Tragically, the same popularity and symbolism made the World Trade Center a target for those who wished America harm. Years before Osama bin Laden and al-Qaeda trained their sights on the World Trade Center as part of the 9/11 attacks, Islamic extremists who would later become associated with key al-Qaeda associates like Khalid Sheikh Mohammed committed the first terrorist attack against the Twin Towers with a truck bomb in 1993.

Ramzi Yousef was the mastermind of the plot, and he arranged financing from his uncle, Khalid Sheikh Mohammed, who would eventually become the third-ranking official in al-Qaeda and the mastermind of 9/11. Another key figure in the 1993 plot was Sheik Omar Abdel Rahman, a blind Muslim cleric with radical anti-American views.

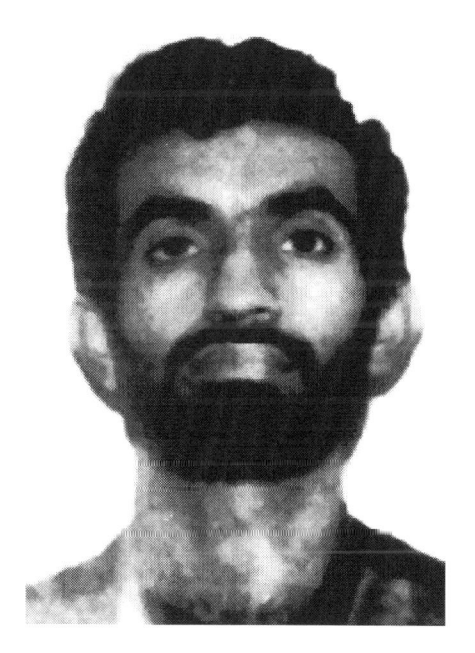

Yousef

Although the 1993 plot was never coordinated with bin Laden's group, many of the conspirators had trained in al-Qaeda training camps in Afghanistan. Yousef himself arrived from Pakistan in 1992 and began building a 1,500 bomb. Yousef intended for the bomb to topple the North Tower into the South Tower, destroying both buildings. When he was injured in a car crash, he even ordered chemicals for the bomb from his hospital room.

The greatest threat to the plot came when one of Rahman's followers, El Sayyid Nosair, was arrested for murdering controversial rabbi Meir Kahane after a speech in New York City. Police found dozens of Arabic language bomb-making manuals and other documents related to terrorist plots, as well as nearly 1,500 rounds of ammunition. However, police were not able to unravel the conspiracy.

Shortly before the attack, Ramzi Yousef mailed letters to New York newspapers with a list of demands, including an end to aid to Israel and an end to American meddling in the internal affairs of Arab countries. The letters promised that the city would suffer a series of terrorist attacks if the demands were not met.

On February 26, 1993, Yousef and co-conspirator Eyad Ismoil, drove a rented van containing the bomb into the public parking garage beneath the North Tower. Yousef lit a 20 foot fuse and the two fled.

The bomb detonated 20 minutes later. While the bomb failed to topple the North Tower, it blew a 30 foot hole through concrete on four sub-levels of the North Tower. The attack crippled the World Trade Center's electrical system, stranding hundreds in elevators. Six people were killed, and smoke rose up to the 93rd floor on both towers. Over 1,000 people were injured.

Tom Hayes, writing for the *Associated Press,* reported, "An explosion apparently caused by a car bomb in an underground garage rocked the 110-story World Trade Center on Friday, killing at least five people, injuring 600 and forcing thousands to flee down dark, smoke filled stairs. A pregnant woman was plucked off the roof of one of the two towers by a helicopter. About 200 kindergartners and elementary school children were stranded for hours on the observation deck. Other people were trapped in elevators, or in rubble in the garage and a train station beneath it. Hundreds poured out of the towers into the streets of lower Manhattan, gasping, their faces black with soot, after groping their way from as high as the 105th floor. Others on upper floors stayed put to await help, and broke windows as the smoke reached them. Eight disabled people were trapped for nine hours on the 94th floor before they were taken to the roof and removed by helicopter, the last people out of the building, the Port Authority said. In all, 23 people were rescued from the towers by helicopter. The towers, the world's second-largest buildings, shuddered with the noontime explosion. Thick black smoke billowed in minutes to the top of both buildings, where some 130,000 people work or visit each day. The blast created a 200-foot-by-100- foot crater six stories deep in the parking garage, witnesses said."

Debris found following the 1993 explosion

It did not take long for people to claim they had done the terrible deed. The article continued, "A terrorist task force of federal and city investigators believed that a car bomb caused the blast, James Fox, an assistant director of the FBI who heads its New York office, told The New York Times. He said no bomb fragments had been found. After the blast, authorities received at least nine telephone calls claiming responsibility, said Jack Killorin, spokesman for the Bureau of Alcohol, Tobacco and Firearms in Washington."

Despite the serious damage inflicted, the bomb could have done far worse damage. Yousef's plan to topple the North Tower might have succeeded if he had parked the van closer to the World Trade Center's foundations, and many more people would have been killed had the attack come earlier or later in the day. Some still speculate that Yousef's original target that day may have been the United Nations, and that the truck bomb was eventually driven to the World Trade Center as a backup plan.

In the wake of the attack, security was increased at the World Trade Center to protect against car and truck bombs. Barriers were introduced to keep cars and trucks further away from the buildings, and cars were not allowed to enter certain areas underneath the towers. In addition, evacuation procedures were vastly improved, and these procedures were in place during 9/11.

Although his conspirators were quickly arrested in the United States, Yousef flew to Pakistan a few hours after the attack and escaped. Yousef eventually made his way to the Philippines, where he worked on other terrorist plots with Khalid Sheikh Mohammed. Coincidentally, the two terrorists were working in the Philippines at the same time Terry Nichols, a convicted conspirator in the Oklahoma City bombing, visited the Philippines. The coincidence led some to wonder whether the two had any ties to Nichols, Timothy McVeigh, and the Oklahoma City bombing, but no ties have ever been discovered.

After Yousef inadvertently started a fire in his apartment, authorities investigating the blaze found bomb-making components. When authorities began closing in on Yousef and Khalid Sheikh Mohammed, the two men fled back to Pakistan. Yousef was eventually arrested in Pakistan and returned to the United States, but Khalid Sheikh Mohammed eluded capture. Yousef remains imprisoned at the "Supermax" prison in Colorado.

Chapter 9: There Will Be No Forgetting September the 11th

"Time is passing. Yet, for the United States of America, there will be no forgetting September the 11th. We will remember every rescuer who died in honor. We will remember every family that lives in grief. We will remember the fire and ash, the last phone calls, the funerals of the children." - President George W. Bush

Shortly after the attack in 1993, most of the work to repair the damage done was completed, and New Yorkers remained cautious but optimistic that the new security measure put in place following the attack would keep them safe in the future. For a while, it looked like they were right, as life went on for a number of years with little interruption. In fact, the work done at the Trade Center so faded into the backdrop of New York City that in the days leading up to September 11, 2001, there was practically no mention of the buildings at all in the press.

September 11, 2001 started as a typical Tuesday morning in New York City, with clear skies. People were still heading to work across Manhattan, including taking trains to the World Trade Center. At 8:46 a.m., people on the streets heard the throttle of a passenger jet overhead but had no reason to pay any attention to it until they heard an extremely loud explosion. The first hijacked plane, American Airlines Flight 11, had just struck the North Tower of the World Trade Center.

Immediately after the first plane hit the North Tower, before it was even clear what had happened, both buildings began to be evacuated. However, on the floors above the plane's impact, no one could evacuate because the plane's impact had destroyed all three emergency stairwells. With smoke and fire spreading, many of the people trapped in the North Tower headed toward windows.

Less than two minutes after the crash, a news crew which had been reporting on the mayoral primary elections for WNYW broadcast the first pictures of the crash. The reporter, Dick Oliver, informed viewers:

"Jim, just a few moments ago something believed to be a plane crashed into the South Tower of the World Trade Center. I just saw flames inside. You can see the smoke coming out of the tower. We have no idea what it was. It was a tremendous boom just a few moments ago. You can hear around me emergency vehicles heading towards the scene. Now this could have been an aircraft or it could have been something internal. It appears to be something coming from the outside, due the nature of the opening on about the 100th floor of the South Tower of the World Trade Center." The reporter, Oliver, had mistaken the South Tower for the North Tower and later corrected himself.

Initial media reports were confused about whether a plane had hit the World Trade Center or whether the explosion occurred internally, but some witnesses claimed to have seen a plane hit the North Tower. CNN broke into a commercial with the headline "World Trade Center disaster", a live shot of the North Tower on fire, and no further information.

Firefighters began to arrive at the World Trade Center by 8:50 a.m. and set up a command post in the lobby of the North Tower. From there, firefighters and other personnel were sent up into the North Tower to find people and evacuate the building. At 9:00 a.m., the chief of the New York Fire Department, Peter Ganci, arrived and ordered that the command post be moved across the street due to falling debris.

The first responders were also hampered by damage done to the North Tower's emergency repeater system, which was required for first responders' radio sets to work correctly. Due to the ongoing fire in the tower, the system malfunctioned, leaving firefighters unable to communicate with the command post or coordinate their actions with other firefighters or the police department.

In the South Tower, a building-wide announcement was made on the public address system at 8:55 a.m., calling the building "secure" and advising occupants to go back to their offices. Many occupants of the South Tower had already evacuated, and others who could obviously see something was terribly wrong ignored the announcement and evacuated anyway.

Of all the horrific images captured during the morning of September 11, 2001, few were as spellbinding or gut-wrenching as the live footage of United Airlines Flight 175 slamming into the South Tower. When American Airlines Flight 11 slammed into the North Tower at 8:46 a.m., it was initially thought a plane may have accidentally crashed into it, and many New Yorkers were familiar with a similar accident involving the Empire State Building several decades earlier. However, as national media outlets started carrying live footage of the damaged North Tower and began speculating as to what happened, they caught Flight 175 directly approaching the South Tower and slamming straight into it at 9:03 a.m.

Just before the second plane hit the South Tower, the New York Fire Department (FDNY) Battalion Chief ordered the North Tower to be evacuated. Due to the confusion and ongoing evacuation of the North Tower, some news reporters and people on site were initially unaware that a second plane had hit the South Tower, initially believing the explosion was a result of the fire in the North Tower.

Local news anchors at WABC, whose live feed of the South Tower was obscured by the North Tower initially speculated that the second explosion was a result of the first plane's fuselage exploding in the fire in the North Tower. After being corrected by witnesses that it was a second plane crashing into the South Tower, the anchors still continued to speculate that a rare navigational system malfunction might have caused similar accidents.

Since the World Trade Center had broadcast the signal for many local television and radio stations, the impacts of the two planes took many of them off the air. Local station WPIX's feed was disrupted by the second plane hitting the South Tower; at the time WPIX was broadcasting a live shot of the World Trade Center and as a result, a frozen image of the second hijacked plane hitting the South Tower was all the station broadcast for several hours.

As horrible as it was, the death toll at Ground Zero could have been far worse. Flight 175 struck the South Tower between floors 77 and 85, considerably lower than Flight 11 had hit the North Tower. While that could have conceivably trapped far more people than those stuck in the North Tower, Flight 175 also hit the South Tower at an angle, as the hijacker pilot banked the plane into the South Tower. Due to this angle, one of the three emergency staircases remained intact for evacuation, unlike in the North Tower. While many used that staircase, it quickly filled with smoke. As a result, many people believed the stairwell was impassable and did not evacuate the building.

The fires and smoke, especially in the North Tower, where no possible evacuation route existed for those above the plane's impact, caused many people to leap from the towers to their deaths. Of the many images that Americans have come to associate with the 9/11 attacks, the images of people jumping out of the World Trade Center to their deaths were particularly disturbing. Nearly 200 people are estimated to have jumped out of the towers before they collapsed, and the media stopped showing images of them shortly after 9/11 due to complaints.

One jumper, known as The Falling Man, was photographed falling upside down going head first, seemingly accepting his fate. Although his identity was never confirmed, some believe it was Jonathon Briley, an asthmatic who worked at the Windows on the World restaurant near the top of the North Tower. The jumpers faced certain death upon impact, but they also posed a threat to people on the ground. Firefighter Daniel Suhr was at street level when a person who had jumped from the North Tower landed on him, killing him.

First responders and other authorities began arriving at the World Trade Center within five minutes of Flight 11 hitting the North Tower, allowing rescue efforts to begin almost immediately. At first, the focus was on evacuating the floors immediately above and below the fires, which was the FDNY's standard procedure in a high-rise fire. However, firefighters soon determined that all three evacuation stairwells were blocked by the fires raging in the impact zone, and that those above the impact of the plane were trapped. Evacuating people by helicopter from the top of the towers was also impossible for a variety of reasons.

The building authorities themselves called initially for a complete evacuation of both the North and the South Tower, but the building authorities halted the evacuation of the South Tower just before Flight 175 struck it, believing the building was safe from the fire in the North Tower. Thankfully, many people in the South Tower ignored the advice of the building authorities to return to their offices. In particular, Morgan Stanley's security officer, Rick Rescoria, a Vietnam War veteran, ignored the building authorities and evacuated Morgan Stanley's offices anyway. When the second plane hit the South Tower, Morgan Stanley was already mostly evacuated. Of its 2,700 employees at work in the South Tower on 9/11, only six died. Four of those 6 were Rescoria and three deputies; they returned to the South Tower after evacuating to assist in evacuating others from the building.

In the North Tower, firefighters, NYPD officers, Port Authority officers and emergency medical technicians were all attempting to evacuate building occupants; however, their efforts were hampered by their radio systems, which were incompatible with each other. As a result, each agency duplicated the efforts of the others, meaning that some offices were checked as many as four times for occupants.

Making matters worse, the fire and the plane's impact had damaged the radio repeater system that the firefighters relied on to communicate with each other and with their commanders. When the second hijacked plane hit the South Tower, the problems in the North Tower were repeated there. NYPD officers could communicate with each other due to their more advanced radio systems, but firefighters could not. This played a major role in the death of more than 300 firefighters, while fewer than 30 NYPD officers were killed in the attacks.

By 9:51 a.m., nearly an hour after Flight 175 had crashed into the South Tower, FDNY firefighters had managed to get to the impact zone in the South Tower. Leading this team of firefighters were Battalion Chief Orio Palmer and Fire Marshall Ronald Bucca. Both took the last working elevator to the 44th floor and raced up the last 34 flights to get to the impact zone.

At the time, Palmer, Bucca, and other firefighters were unaware of warnings called in by those stranded at the top the South Tower. Several 911 callers reported the 105th and 106th floors were collapsing, and police helicopters radioed that the South Tower appeared unstable from above. Although the firefighters had no idea about the South Tower's instability these warnings did reach NYPD officers and Port Authority officers, and many of them evacuated the South Tower.

At the 78th floor, Palmer radioed that the ceiling had collapsed and was open to the 79th floor, and that there were many dead bodies. Later investigations found that after the first evacuation of the South Tower was stopped via the public address system, many people congregated in the

South Tower's "sky lobbies", from which they could take elevators back to their offices or out of the building. The 78th floor, the site of the impact, was a sky lobby and the bodies Palmer reported were those who had waited to see whether they would be evacuated again or permitted to return to work.

At 9:56 a.m., a few minutes after Palmer reported reaching the impact zone at the South Tower, the entire South Tower collapsed in the span of a just a few seconds, 56 minutes after Flight 175 hit it. Initially, media outlets and those not close to the scene believed that a new explosion or plane impact had produced a dust cloud hiding the South Tower. But it soon became clear that the South Tower was no longer standing, an event that people could have never imagined even after the planes had hit the towers. Battalion Chief Palmer and Fire Marshall Bucca were among those killed in the collapse.

Immediately after the collapse of the South Tower, NYPD and other first responders other than firefighters pulled back from the North Tower as well. Although radio commands were given to pull back from the North Tower by commanders, most firefighters in the North Tower never received the order. The commands were radioed at least twice, but most firefighters never heard them due to the failing radio repeater system in the building. Furthermore, dust and smoke likely obscured any view of the South Tower's collapse by firefighters in the North Tower. As a result, most firefighters killed in the North Tower, like Palmer and Bucca in the South Tower, were unaware that they were running out of time. The total collapse of a high-rise was not usually considered in firefighter training; the strategy in high-rise fires was to evacuate people or move them to safe floors and then try to control the fire.

At 10:28 a.m., the North Tower collapsed, 100 minutes after Flight 11 hit it. The emergency stairwells that were to be used to evacuate the North Tower had been destroyed by the impact of the plane, so no one above the impact zone in the North Tower survived the attack. As a result, everyone at work on September 11 in several businesses at the top of the North Tower perished, and one of the hardest hit companies was Cantor Fitzgerald, an investment bank that lost all 658 employees who were at its headquarters at the top of the North Tower on September 11, 2001. These employees represented about 66% of Cantor Fitzgerald's workforce.

Shortly after the second hijacked plane hit the South Tower, when it was apparent that New York City was suffering terrorist attacks, all bridges and tunnels into Manhattan were closed, literally leaving everyone on the island stranded. Most high-profile buildings and high rise buildings in New York City and elsewhere were also being evacuated, including the United Nations, the Empire State Building, the Sears Tower in Chicago, the Mall of America near Minneapolis, and the U.S. Bank Tower in Los Angeles.

Naturally, in New York City the evacuation included most of the buildings in Lower Manhattan. The NYPD determined that the combination of the ongoing response to the collapse of the Twin Towers and the threat of more terrorism made Lower Manhattan too dangerous for large numbers of civilians standing outside of their office buildings. In response to those concerns, New York City Mayor Rudy Giuliani ordered Lower Manhattan evacuated entirely.

Despite the evacuation order, evacuating millions of people who worked and lived in Lower Manhattan on any given weekday would not have been easy under normal circumstances, let alone 9/11. With the collapse of the Twin Towers, the PATH station that allowed New Jersey commuters to board trains back to New Jersey was destroyed. In addition, two Lower Manhattan subway stations were damaged by the collapse of the towers. Thus, neither the PATH nor the subway could help evacuate Lower Manhattan.

Moreover, motor vehicles could not use the closed bridges to leave the island. As a result, people who drove into the Lower Manhattan that morning were unable to drive out. Even if the bridges hadn't been closed, many people's cars were destroyed in the attacks or did not have their keys because the parking attendants who had them had already begun evacuating themselves.

Immediately after the dust cleared on the collapsed towers, first responders got into the debris to begin looking for survivors. In a span of minutes, the mission had switched from evacuation to rescue and recovery, setting off frantic searches across 16 acres of wreckage for survivors. The towers' collapse had also badly damaged all of the vehicles and equipment on site as well, and without any undamaged construction equipment available, first responders and volunteers were forced to remove debris by hand. The rescue effort was also hampered by concerns about the stability of surrounding buildings, and work was frequently stopped to ensure that no neighboring building was in danger of collapsing.

By the afternoon of 9/11, volunteer medical workers had set up a makeshift hospital a few blocks from the World Trade Center site. However, by September 12, it became clear that there were few survivors of the collapse so the hospital was closed down. In the 48 hours after the attacks, only 11 survivors were pulled out of the rubble.

Before 9/11, "ground zero" referred to the spot on the ground directly below the detonation of a nuclear weapon. The term "zero" was code in the Manhattan project for the spot chosen for the first nuclear test, and ground zero was closely associated with complete devastation. However, after the collapse of the World Trade Center on 9/11, several national media outlets were referring to the site of the World Trade Center as "Ground Zero." The phrase was already being used immediately after the collapse of the towers, an apt reference to the widespread ash and debris that made those who experienced it think of nuclear fallout when trying to describe it.

Ground Zero also aptly described what rescue workers and reporters were seeing at the World Trade Center site after the towers collapsed. With the entire World Trade Center complex destroyed, the wreckage spread across several square acres. And despite Mayor Rudolph Giuliani's attempt to assure people that the air was safe to breathe, the enormous amount of dust that was released by the collapse of the towers made Ground Zero hard to even approach on September 11 and 12. For days afterward, the thick dust made breathing difficult in Lower Manhattan without a mask, and the collapse of the towers resulted in the largest release of asbestos in history, instantly leading to worries that people near the area would suffer respiratory problems.

Although the site largely became known as Ground Zero, members of the rescue teams and the workers trying the clear the debris from the site did not use the term "Ground Zero", preferring instead to call the site "The Pile". The term referred to the enormous pile of debris left by the collapse of the Twin Towers. Since the rescue teams were working around the clock in 12 hour shifts and sleeping on-site, they had little exposure to the media's terminology and had developed their own terms to describe the landscape they worked in.

The collapse of the Twin Towers released the largest amount of asbestos in history and produced an enormous amount of fine dust that covered all of Lower Manhattan and remained in the air for weeks after the attacks. In the days after the 9/11 attacks, both Mayor Giuliani and the federal Environmental Protection Agency pronounced the air safe. Although Mayor Giuliani and the EPA tried to assure New Yorkers that the air was safe to breathe, many feared that exposure to the area would cause respiratory problems. Indeed, immediately after the collapse of the Twin Towers, rescue workers, reporters and civilians on site noticed that the dust made it difficult to breathe, and some rescue workers even reported coughing up blood after their 12 hour shifts on "the Pile".

For most aspects of the cleanup, Mayor Giuliani took control of the effort from federal agencies and placed it in control of a little-known city office. Investigators later found that the city did not enforce regulations requiring the use of protective respirators at the World Trade Center site, and that few respirators were available for workers to use. Furthermore, according to later reports, the local office of the EPA refused sophisticated equipment from the agency's regional branch, and instead used a less sensitive test to determine if the dust contained cancer-causing asbestos. Over 100 people are estimated to have died as a result of inhaling dust from the collapse of the towers. One first responder who spent months at the World Trade Center site developed advanced lung cancer at 37, even though he had never had cancer before and did not smoke.

In the days after 9/11, thousands of volunteers from across the country came to New York City to help with the rescue efforts. The volunteers included construction personnel, especially ironworkers and those skilled in operating heavy equipment, firefighters, doctors, emergency medical technicians, and police officers. Rescue teams skilled in finding survivors beneath rubble came from all over the country, and over 400 search dogs were used. Unfortunately, the rescue effort was not as successful as many hoped because so few survived the collapse of the towers.

The extent of the tragedy of the 9/11 attacks shocked Americans who witnessed the death of thousands of innocent people on live television when the towers collapsed. Initial speculation about the death toll ranged as high as 50,000, based on the fact that 250,000 were known to either work at or visit the World Trade Center every day. Ultimately, it was determined that about 3,000 people were killed in the terrorist attacks.

After searching for hours for survivors in the rubble of the World Trade Center collapse, Dan McWilliams, a firefighter, spotted an American flag on a yacht docked in the Hudson River, The flag was hanging from a broken wooden flag pole. McWilliams took the flag and walked it back to the World Trade Center site, where he and two of his friends, also firefighters, planned to plant the wooden pole in the ground. But then they found a larger flagpole sticking out of the debris at a 45 degree angle. While raising the flag on this flag pole, a photographer for the New York Times snapped what would become an iconic picture. The picture ran in the September 13, 2001 edition of the paper, and it was immediately noted for its eerie similarities to the iconic image of Marines raising the flag on Iwo Jima during World War II.

On September 12, 2001, another flag was found amid the wreckage of the World Trade Center that would also become a part of an enduring commemoration of the attacks and a symbol of America rebuilding. Firefighters noticed a large, tattered flag wrapped around scaffolding near the World Trade Center site. The flag, which had been severely damaged, could not be retrieved for safety reasons for several weeks. Eventually the flag, which was injured but survived the attacks, flew over the rescue workers and became a powerful symbol of America's strength to survive such a terrible strategy.

The most well known memorial was the one that gave Americans a visual reminder of the World Trade Center's Twin Towers. After 9/11, Manhattan's skyline was hauntingly empty, serving as a painful reminder of the 9/11 attacks and where the Twin Towers once stood.

New York City's empty skyline was the setting for a moving tribute to 9/11 victims beginning on March 11, 2002, the six month anniversary of the attacks. With enough debris having been removed at that point, 88 searchlights were installed near the former base of the two towers in two groups. When illuminated, the searchlights formed two beams of light that symbolized the missing towers. The project was called "Tribute in Light." The two beams of light were re-lit on September 11, 2002, marking the one year anniversary of the attacks, and this memorial continued every year on the anniversary of the attacks.

President George W. Bush visited the World Trade Center site on September 14, 2001. When rescue workers cheered his arrival and began chanting "USA! USA!," President Bush borrowed a bullhorn from a worker and began giving a short impromptu speech. As Bush began speaking, one rescue worker yelled, "I can't hear you!" Bush responded, "I can hear you. The rest of the world hears you. And the people who knocked these buildings down will hear all of us soon."

Chapter 10: Considering a Replacement

"A long year has passed since enemies attacked our country. ... For all Americans, it has been a year of adjustment, of coming to terms with the difficult knowledge that our Nation has determined enemies and that we are not invulnerable to their attacks. Yet, in the events that have challenged us, we have also seen the character that will deliver us. ... September the 11th, 2001, will always be a fixed point in the life of America. The loss of so many lives left us to examine our own. Each of us was reminded that we are here only for a time and these counted days should be filled with things that last and matter: Love for our families, love for our neighbors, and for our country; gratitude for life and to the Giver of life. We resolved a year ago to honor every last person lost. We owe them remembrance, and we owe them more. We owe them and their children, and our own, the most enduring monument we can build, a world of liberty and security made possible by the way America leads and by the way Americans lead our lives. ... America has entered a great struggle that tests our strength and, even more, our resolve. Our Nation is patient and steadfast. ... Now and in the future, Americans will live as free people, not in fear and never at the mercy of any foreign plot or power." - President George W. Bush, September 11, 2002

In the wake of 9/11, rebuilding the heart of New York quickly became synonymous with rebuilding the nation's heart. In an address to a joint session of Congress on September 20, 2001, President Bush observed, to thundering applause, "My fellow citizens, for the last nine days, the entire world has seen for itself the state of our Union -- and it is strong. ... I thank the Congress for its leadership at such an important time. All of America was touched on the evening of the tragedy to see Republicans and Democrats joined together on the steps of this Capitol, singing 'God Bless America.' And you did more than sing; you acted, by delivering $40 billion to rebuild our communities and meet the needs of our military. ... Tonight we welcome two leaders who embody the extraordinary spirit of all New Yorkers: Governor George Pataki, and Mayor Rudolph Giuliani. As a symbol of America's resolve, my administration will work with Congress, and these two leaders, to show the world that we will rebuild New York City. ...this country will define our times, not be defined by them. As long as the United States of America is determined and strong, this will not be an age of terror; this will be an age of liberty, here and across the world."

Pataki

Giuliani

While the nation still mourned, the Lower Manhattan Development Corporation, the owner of the original towers and the land they were built on, began to plan. Before even a year had passed, its headquarters announced on August 14, 2002, "The Lower Manhattan Development Corporation today extended an invitation to the most innovative architects and planners around the world to participate in an LMDC design study regarding the future of the World Trade Center site and surrounding areas. New York New Visions, a coalition of 21 architecture, engineering, planning, landscape architecture and design organizations, will advise LMDC in selecting up to five teams to prepare additional concept plans for the next phase of the planning process. The teams selected will receive a stipend from the LMDC and be guided by new, flexible program alternatives developed in conjunction with the Port Authority of New York and New Jersey. Since the six initial plans were released in July, the LMDC and Port Authority have received 5000 suggestions via email through the RenewNYC.com website, comments from over 5000 participants at the Listening To The City town hall forums, comments from thousands of visitors to the exhibit of the plans at Federal Hall and additional input from LMDC's eight Advisory Councils. Public input indicates a strong desire for an inclusive planning process, as well as consensus around key goals for rebuilding."

The press release went on to add, "The following ideas will be incorporated into new program alternatives, which will be finalized upon selection of the five teams in September:

Distinctive Skyline
New York City lost a critical part of its identity when the World Trade Center towers were destroyed. A tall symbol or structure that would be recognized around the world is crucial to restoring the spirit of the city.

Preference for Recognition of the Tower Footprints
Based on public input, there is a preference for preserving the footprints of the Twin Towers for memorial space and precluding commercial development on those locations.

Commercial and Retail Space
The Port Authority and LMDC will develop various options for a mixture of commercial and retail space on and/or off the site. These options will establish minimum and maximum square footage for mixed-use development to direct the planners. The ranges of space will be developed prior to the selection of the five teams.

Grand Promenade on West Street
Connect the future World Trade Center memorial with the ferries in Battery Park to Liberty and Ellis Islands. This grand promenade could reinvent West Street as a wide public boulevard and living memorial and might include depressing some or all of West Street south of Vesey Street.

New Street Grid
Partially restore the street grid within the former World Trade Center site, which integrates walking and/or driving routes on and to the site.

Central Transit Center
Create an integrated transit center serving Lower Manhattan for PATH and subway passengers. A grand and visible station is needed to orient travelers and provide a

spectacular point of arrival for commuters, tourists, and residents.

Residential Housing
There is significant demand for residential housing in Lower Manhattan. Planners will explore the possibility of residential housing on and off the site.

Cultural Elements
Utilize the unique opportunity for building major cultural institutions or a complex. Sites for a museum, performing arts center, or other spaces should be part of the plan.

Sequence of Public Open Spaces of Different Sizes
In addition to the main memorial space, plans should include public open spaces, eg. parks and plazas, of different sizes and configurations."

Due to the delicate nature of the nation's feelings on the subject of rebuilding, LMDC President Louis Tomson assured people, "At Listening to the City and other public forums throughout the last several months, we vowed to incorporate public input into the planning process. The invaluable public input we received is helping to shape the future of downtown. Involving additional design teams and allowing greater flexibility in the program will ensure that a variety of bold options will be introduced during this second phase." Joseph Seymour, then the Executive Director of the Port Authority, which would be working hand in hand with the LMDC, insisted, "The input from family members of September 11th heroes, from residents and other stakeholders, has been extremely valuable. Based on that input, we are now able to take the next step in refining plans for the World Trade Center site and surrounding areas. These plans have enormous emotional significance for the Port Authority, New York City and for our nation. We have been listening carefully. The time has come to incorporate what we have heard into the planning process."

Chapter 11: Competition

"All the architects in the competition were required to include a tall element in their designs, and Libeskind chose neither a super-tall office building, which would have been difficult to rent and probably impossible to finance, nor a pure, Eiffel Tower-like symbol, which would have been far too expensive to build without some offsetting income. His notion, developed with the structural engineer Irwin Cantor, was that the tall spire and the office building would share a structural system and an elevator core. This was both practical and visually powerful. But Libeskind has had to contend with a host of critics, the most severe of whom has been Herbert Muschamp of the New York Times, who, after initially praising his scheme as 'a perfect balance between aggression and desire,' turned vociferously against it in the weeks before the final selection. He called it 'stunted,' 'predictably kitsch,' and 'demagogic.' The New York Post published an editorial titled 'Control Freak,' which referred to Libeskind as 'self-promoting' and 'bizarre' and suggested that he should have no influence at all in deciding what should be built at Ground Zero." - Paul Goldberger, "Urban Warriors," *The New Yorker*, September 15, 2003

    Unfortunately, the first group of designs submitted failed to impress the judges, so the selection process was begun again, this time with a deadline of mid-December 2002. Nine firms submitted designs that were deemed acceptable, and on December 19, the *Associated Press* reported, "Nine competing designs for the World Trade Center site were unveiled Wednesday, with several of them boldly proposing that the city answer the Sept. 11 terrorist attack by erecting the tallest skyscrapers on Earth. Four of the plans for ground zero call for topping Malaysia's 1,483-foot Petronas Twin Towers. One envisions a 2,100-foot skyscraper, while another proposes a 1,776-foot tower topped with a spire.' The article also observed, 'The plans for rebuilding the site and surrounding neighborhood came from seven teams of architects from Berlin. London, Amsterdam. Tokyo, New York and Los Angeles, and were selected from 407 submissions. One team whose drawings were chosen submitted three plans. A first set of plans released in July was derided as boring and overstuffed with office space. The new proposals take a variety of approaches to the 16-acre site. They include towers that 'kiss' and gardens in the sky. 'These are designs not only for our time but for all time,' said John Whitehead, chairman of the Lower Manhattan Development Corp. 'They must transcend the present, to speak to our children and to their children ... to send an immortal message.' One of the plans suggests five 1,111-foot skyscrapers, connected by arches. 'In my view, taller is not better,' said the plan's architect, Richard Meier, who designed the Getty Museum in Los Angeles. 'Everybody who builds the tallest building in the world has it for about 15 seconds.' London-based Foster and Partners proposed a unique 'twinned tower,' a 1,764-foot skyscraper that would divide into two parts but 'kiss' at three points to create public space and observation decks."

A picture of the Freedom Tower's spire taken by Vlad Lazarenko

From its very inception, everyone involved understood that the Freedom Tower would be only one part of a larger complex designed to, more than anything else, honor those who died. However, none of the other buildings would have either the symbolic or actual importance of One World Trade Center itself.

The architects designing the new building were facing a challenge unlike anything they had dealt with before; in addition to building a skyscraper; they were building the world's largest memorial to a murdered population. This aspect of the task was constantly in the forefront of the project, as the *AP* article noted: "Gov. George Pataki praised the plans, saying they 'really reflect what we want to show the world.' However, victims' relatives said it was hard to imagine anyone wanting to work in skyscrapers there, or even look up at them. 'Initially, I have to say it does bother me, but that's a reality that we'll have to come to grips with,' said Bruce DeCell, whose son-in-law worked on the 92nd floor of the trade center's north tower. 'Hopefully these towers will be built with the proper technology because of the skepticism that has emerged now about taller buildings.'"

As the judges looked over the plans, one architect seemed to have gotten the message better than the others. Daniel Libeskind, born in Poland to Holocaust survivors, had lived with his parents in Israel for two years before moving to New York. A musical prodigy, he gave up playing altogether while still very young, and in high school, he developed an interest in mathematics that eventually led him to architecture, even though it was not "cool." He explained, "Architecture was considered very lowly at Bronx Science. If you were really smart, you did quantum physics. I didn't take it that way, as only doing doors and windows, but I didn't know what architects did. Had I known that most architects were people in white shirts sitting at desks designing details of buildings no one would take responsibility for, then I never would have become an architect. Architecture was once a humanistic pursuit. It is not just functional diagrams of an office or a shopping center."

Ishmael Orendain's picture of Libeskind

As a child, Libeskind had watched the Twin Towers being built. In speaking of his drawing for Freedom Tower, he proclaimed, "A skyscraper rises above its predecessors, restoring the spiritual peak of the city, creating an icon that speaks to our vitality in the face of danger and our optimism in the aftermath of tragedy."

As he grew up, Libeskind's work was good enough to earn him a scholarship to Cooper Union, where he fell under the mentorship of John Hejduk, the dean of the architecture school. Eventually, he was offered a job with the prestigious Richard Meier firm. However, his employment there did not last, and he left the well-paying job to pursue his own interests, including Nina Lewis, whom he married in 1969. She later recalled, "I arranged for a trip to the Caribbean, but Daniel had got a travel scholarship to see the work of Frank Lloyd Wright, and that became our honeymoon. Neither of us could drive, so we went with two other students. One was a strict Lutheran, the other a Jehovah's Witness, and neither of them was what you would call loose and easy. We camped out in sleeping bags in a station wagon. That was when I realized my life would never be normal."

Hejduk

Libeskind's plan for the new World Trade Center, called "Life Victorious," won over the judges and ultimately the competition. According to a 2003 article in *The New Yorker*, "Most people who have come to know Libeskind in New York refer to him as 'they,' meaning him and his wife, Nina, who is his business partner, office manager, strategist, negotiator, publicist, and nearly constant companion. They are both slight, and both have short, closely cropped gray hair and wear glasses. Nina is present at almost every meeting her husband attends, and when he isn't there she represents their firm, Studio Daniel Libeskind. After they won the competition in February, Nina…negotiated contracts worth nearly six million dollars from the L.M.D.C. and the

Port Authority, for work on the master plan, the design guidelines, and the memorial areas of Ground Zero. ... Each day started with a fax from Nina's assistant in Berlin that laid out that day's schedule of meetings. 'Nina has a great technique,' Daniel said to me. 'I don't know my schedule in advance—if I knew what I had to do each day I couldn't do it.' Nina Libeskind sees her job as keeping the pressures of the world away from her husband so that he is free to think and draw. 'Daniel can spend days, literally days, thinking about doorknobs,' Nina says."

Chapter 12: Controversy

"No other steel building—if it hadn't been knocked over—had ever fallen like that. ... There were an awful lot of people who thought we shouldn't build anything. Then there was another group—almost as large—who thought it should be exactly like it was. People felt a loss in the skyline. The only thing we could do as a nation was to rebuild exactly what was there? Not very adventuresome. So I thought the idea was to solve some problems [by putting] back the street grid, which we did, in fact ensure by the building of Seven WTC. ...the most iconic buildings are the ones that [are] really simple in form and shouldn't be fussy. ... The idea was that anybody visiting downtown New York on their spring break could go back to their ninth-grade class and draw that building very simply—like the Washington Monument. ... Of all the buildings to be built down there, this is the one that had a relationship to the memorial. Something as simple as that form could be a marker and a memory." - David Childs

If Libeskind expected opposition in building his creation, he certainly got it, primarily in the form of Larry Silverstein, who owned the lease on the original Trade Center, and his associate, David Childs. From the very moment discussions on rebuilding began, Silverstein made it clear that he would have his say in the process. According to the same *New Yorker* article that praised Libeskind, "Silverstein claims to have the right to rebuild the Trade Center. There had been talk of buying him out, or even of condemning the property, but no one— not the Port Authority or Governor Pataki, who theoretically could have—followed up on the idea. Silverstein is the beneficiary of several billion dollars in insurance money that will likely provide most of the funds, at least initially, for construction on the site. When Libeskind's design was chosen, Silverstein said he thought that it was an excellent site plan, but he didn't say much about the Freedom Tower. He intended to do business the way he always had, and he wanted his own architect, David Childs of Skidmore, Owings & Merrill, to design the tower. He also wanted to move it closer to the spot where a new transportation hub will be built. Childs, unlike Libeskind, is an experienced designer of tall buildings, including the AOL Time Warner complex at Columbus Circle, and he has been playing with designs for a tower on the World Trade Center site since late in 2001, long before Libeskind was in the picture."

Childs

As it turned out, Libeskind was more than a match for Silverstein, and the battle lines were soon drawn. The article continued, "Early this summer, Silverstein's money and chutzpah seemed to be getting him what he wanted, but Libeskind, who was born in Poland and grew up in the Bronx, turned out to know more than a little about street fighting in New York. He had hired a lawyer, Edward Hayes, who is a close friend of Governor Pataki, and Hayes argued that the public expected his client to build everything he had envisioned—that his plans had been presented as a package. Libeskind made it clear that he was prepared to walk off the project, which would have embarrassed both the L.M.D.C. and Pataki, whose support was crucial to Libeskind's selection, and who has pledged to start construction on the tower by next year, when the Republicans come to town for their Presidential Convention. He made the pledge in April, standing in front of a six-foot-tall rendering of Libeskind's Freedom Tower."

Soon, even political officials were involved in the controversy, trying hard to find some middle ground for the men to agree on. "Pataki urged Kevin Rampe, the president of the L.M.D.C., to force Libeskind and Childs to sort things out, and Rampe called a meeting at L.M.D.C. headquarters at One Liberty Plaza on July 15th. Libeskind came with Edward Hayes and several staff members. Childs, who said later that he hadn't been told about the draconian aspect of the meeting, brought one of his architectural partners and Janno Lieber, Larry Silverstein's executive in charge of the World Trade Center site. The architects and their entourages sat in separate conference rooms at opposite ends of the twentieth floor, and Rampe and Matthew Higgins, the chief operating officer of the L.M.D.C., shuttled between the two camps. After five hours of this, nobody had budged from his original position. 'The Libeskinds are afraid of being chewed up by the Skidmore, Owings & Merrill machine,' Rampe told Childs. 'Well, I'm afraid of being chewed up by the Libeskind machine,' Childs replied."

At first, it seemed that the two men could never find a middle ground, but eventually they did. "Sometime after nine in the evening, Higgins sent out for pizza, and not long after that Rampe suggested that it might be helpful if Libeskind and Childs discussed things face to face, away from everyone else. The two men went into a third room. Childs was firm. He had a design for a tower and he didn't want Libeskind's design to be the starting point of any collaboration. 'Only if this is a blank slate can I work with you,' he said. 'This is not a tabula rasa,' Libeskind replied. 'The Freedom Tower is an image, a basis.' 'I have my own image,' Childs said. 'I appreciate and respect what you do, but it is not what I do.' Libeskind began to sketch his design on a piece of paper. 'I have an idea how we can develop it,' he insisted, but Childs continued to demur. Libeskind said that he would agree to a fifty-fifty sharing of authority. Childs said that was impossible: 'Someone has to be the writer of the Constitution.' Childs told me later that he felt that Libeskind was wedded to a sculptural image, and that he found his asymmetrical scheme illogical. 'He is shaping a clay block and sticking a sword on one side of it,' Childs said. 'It was gruelling,' Libeskind recalled. 'It felt like the Grand Inquisitor scene in 'The Brothers Karamazov.''"

Ultimately, it was decided that Childs would be the official architect for the project, while Libeskind would "meaningfully collaborate" on the work. Also working with Childs was Julie Hiromoto, a graduate of the Yale School of Architecture who would be something of the environmental conscience of the team. She said, "I think resiliency is really about designing in a way that can be flexible and adaptive to the unknown. We studied a lot of things about the actual geometry of the building, the floor plans and how we would occupy that space. One of the things that was very important to us was to have a column free interior. David [talked] about the structure and the columns being pushed out to the exterior of the building; we have a very strong core in the center. ... Before Seven WTC, you had some very green buildings and some very pretty buildings, and they were always kind of mutually exclusive. There were very few examples that people could come up with that said these are very beautiful buildings that I want to have and green buildings that we should be building."

Seven World Trade Center

For his part, Childs insisted, "We really wanted our design to be grounded in something that was very real, not just in sculptural sketches. We explored the infrastructural challenges because the proper solution would have to be compelling, not just beautiful. The design does have great sculptural implications, and we fully understand the iconic importance of the tower, but it also has to be a highly efficient building. The discourse about Freedom Tower has often been limited to the symbolic, formal and aesthetic aspects but we recognize that if this building doesn't function well, if people don't want to work and visit there, then we will have failed as architects."

Chapter 13: Cornerstone

"To the rebuilders of the World Trade Center site, the 20-ton hunk of granite that will mark the foundation of a 1,776-foot skyscraper today represents promise and progress. An inscribed cornerstone at the southeastern corner of the Freedom Tower's foundation will begin a construction project that officials say will help the city reclaim its skyline, nearly three years after losing the twin towers in the Sept. 11 attacks. But the future of the 16-acre site isn't exactly set in stone. ... Despite the uncertainty, today's ceremony is "an incredible step for the rebuilding of ground zero," said Daniel Libeskind, the designer who conceived the site's original master plan. Construction officially begins today on the Freedom Tower; at 1,776 feet, a height meant to symbolize America's independence, no skyscraper in the world is taller. The 13-year-old son of a Port Authority of New York and New Jersey police officer killed on Sept. 11 will read the Declaration of Independence at today's ceremony. The tower is set to rise in a corner of the site that still holds ruins of a parking garage, although it will be several months before the progress is seen above street level. Crews will spend most of the rest of the year demolishing parts of the garage, removing some sections of it for historic preservation." - Amy Westfeldt, writing for the *Associated Press* on July 4, 2004

On July 4, 2004, assorted dignitaries met in New York to lay the cornerstone for the new Freedom Tower. By this time, nearly three years of time had passed and people were anxious to see some sort of progress in rebuilding the lost towers. However, their wait was far from over, because even after those in charge finally came to an agreement about the building's design, there was still plenty of controversy to come. For instance, many took exception to the fact that the new tower, while taller than the previous two, would have significantly less office space. Also, the new building would have only 82 floors, a limit demanded by Silverstein, who insisted that making the building any taller would make it too much of a target for future attacks. The New York City Police Department also weighed in on the subject, leading to a 187 feet tall concrete base being added to the structure's design in April 2005. This would later be covered with blast-resistant glass and stainless steel. High above the sturdy base, it was decided that the tower would taper gently into a unique, octagonal shape.

Perhaps inevitably, in spite of everyone's best efforts, many people were unhappy with both the design and the progress. Columnist David Shuster weighed in on February 17, 2005, opining, "I consider part of lower Manhattan to be hallowed ground. Nearly 3,000 people lost their lives in the World Trade Center towers — and for that reason alone, our nation should make absolutely sure that what gets built on 'Ground Zero' is an inspiring tribute to all who loved the Twin Towers, worked in them, and died there. For much of the last year, I have been following the twists and turns of the Freedom Tower — the announced office building replacement for the towers destroyed on 9/11. But I regret to report that this proposed skyscraper, instead of standing for freedom, is fast becoming a symbol of incompetence, deceit, political cronyism, and shame."

   Shuster also complained about the design of the building itself, observing, "The Freedom Tower office/skyscraper was designed by architect Daniel Libeskind (who never built a skyscraper before) and embraced by New York Governor George Pataki. ... One of their selling points was that this would be the world's 'tallest building.' But that's only true if you include the hollow windmill turbines, the eccentric spire, and the broadcast antennas. Only 70 stories of the Freedom Tower will be occupied. New York's Empire State building, finished in 1931, is occupied through 102 stories. ... I don't know anybody (aside from friends and family of Daniel Libeskind and George Pataki) who is really excited about the design... not one. Take a look for yourself. Is this design something you are proud of? Does it send the proper message to those who want to terrorize and scare our nation? Consider the major players in New York: Former mayor Rudy Giuliani is not camera shy. But he has been notably absent from nearly everything associated with this project. Mayor Michael Bloomberg seems about as enthusiastic as somebody about to get a root canal. The New York City police and firefighters? Ask them and you will get an earful. Most of New York's 'finest' seem to despise the Freedom Tower."

Bloomberg

From there, Shuster went on to make some not very thinly veiled accusations against those who were involved in the project, especially New York Governor George Pataki: "One of Governor Pataki's most prominent political and financial supporters is a man named Ron Lauder. ... On September 26, 2002, Ron Lauder gave $30,000 to a campaign fundraising committee called 'Friends of Pataki.' On that same day, Sept. 26, 2002, 'Friends of Pataki' received $28,000 from Lauder's wife. On that same day, Sept. 26, 2002, 'Friends of Pataki' received $10,000 from Lauder's daughter. September 26, 2002 was also the day that the Pataki controlled Lower Manhattan Development Corporation quietly narrowed down more than 400 entries in the WTC replacement 'design contest' to seven semi-finalists. One of the semi finalists was a close friend of the Lauder family, an architect named Daniel Libeskind. Did Governor Pataki, in exchange for the Lauder campaign contributions, pressure the LMDC to select a design by Lauder friend Daniel Libeskind? Governor Pataki's office refused to comment and directed me to the Lower Manhattan Development Corporation. A spokesperson for the LMDC called the theories 'bizarre' and said, 'we went through an unprecedented worldwide selection process. Stories that suggest anything to the contrary are absurd.' Regarding the engineering challenges, the LMDC spokesperson said, 'we are working through the process.' None the less, several of my contacts and colleagues in New York say they still don't like the 'smell' coming from the proposed Freedom Tower."

The controversies were finally resolved in the spring of 2006. On April 26, the *Associated Press* reported, "World Trade Center developer Larry Silverstein and government officials agreed Tuesday to most terms of a deal that scales back his role at the site and surrenders his job as landlord of the iconic Freedom Tower, ending four months of messy negotiations over control of ground zero. The rewriting of Silverstein's 99-year lease to the fallen twin towers would give the Port Authority of New York and New Jersey, which owns the site, control of two out of five planned office towers, including the 1,776-foot Freedom Tower that Silverstein has been developing. Silverstein would lease three other towers that are considered to be in more lucrative spots on the 16-acre lower Manhattan site. Officials said the deal ensures all five planned towers would be built by 2012. ... Gov. George Pataki said the plan 'will make certain that the rebuilt World Trade Center will anchor the financial capital of the world and make our nation proud.' Silverstein said at a news conference outside his 1 World Trade Center building next to ground zero that he had some minor objections to the latest offer that could be resolved within days. 'This is about moving the rebuilding forward as quickly as possible,' Silverstein said. 'All the finger-pointing must stop.'"

For the waiting public, the best news lay further down the article, as the writer reported, "The agreement left open the possibility that construction still could begin on the Freedom Tower by the end of the week, which politicians have repeatedly promised. Janno Lieber, a Silverstein company vice president, said 'we can start it tomorrow' if an agreement is reached." While things did not move quite that quickly, the agreement did mark "the end of the beginning," and work on Freedom Tower began in earnest a few months later.

Chapter 14: Construction

"After months of disputes over the future of Ground Zero, state and city officials finally brought in the heavy equipment and began construction Thursday on the 1,776-foot Freedom Tower that will rise at the World Trade Center site. 'It is going to be a symbol of our freedom and independence,' Gov. George Pataki said after three yellow construction trucks driven by workers wearing hard hats emblazoned with the American flag and the words 'Freedom Tower, World Trade Center' rolled down a ramp to applause from politicians. ... The Freedom Tower is scheduled to open in 2011, and officials said Wednesday's deal means all five towers could be built by 2012. Construction has also begun on the memorial. The project will return millions of square feet of office space, shops and people to downtown's financial district. 'Everybody had a smile on their face and everybody understands if you're not happy with the design, you had your chance, if you're not happy with the deal, you had your chance,' Mayor Michael Bloomberg said. 'We've finally all come together and said what we're going to do, so now we're going to do it.' Business and civic leaders have wondered whether there is demand for that much office space downtown, and said that the Freedom Tower has not attracted tenants yet because of its height and it's potential as a terrorist target. But Pataki said: 'We are not going to just build low in the face of a war against terror.'" - Amy Westfeldt, *Associated Press*, April 28, 2006

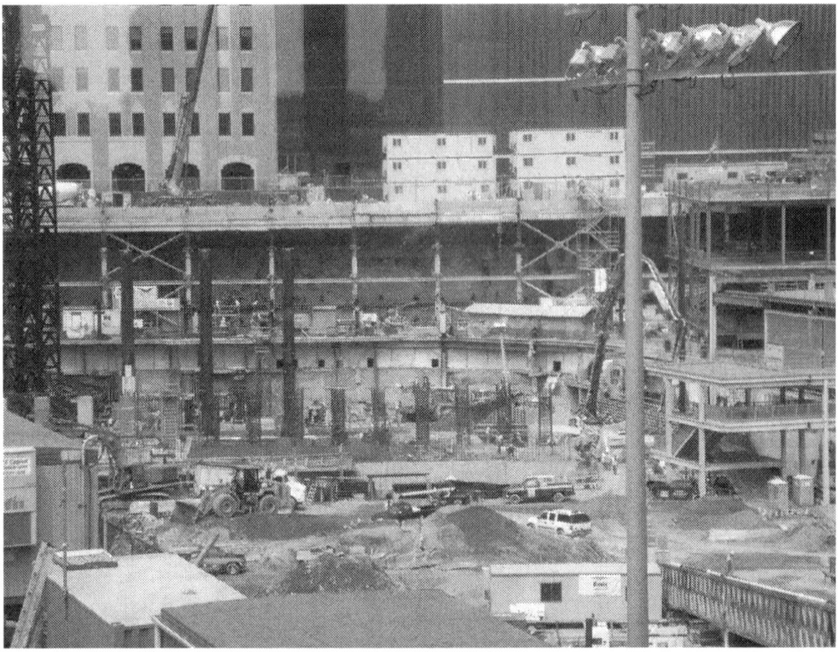

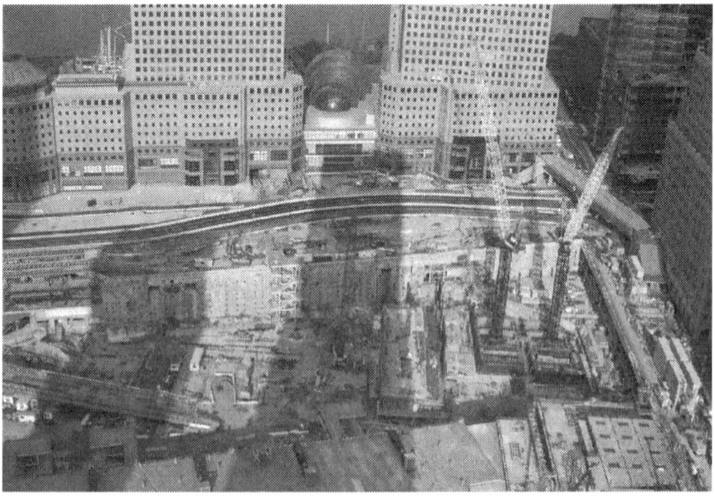

Pictures of the construction in 2007.

On November 18, 2006, after years of delays, arguments and clean-up, the foundation was finally poured for the Freedom Tower. 40 concrete trucks, each carrying 10 cubic yards of mixed concrete backed up to the gash left in the earth by clean-up crews and began pouring. A month later, those most closely touched by the attacks on 9/11 were invited to a special ceremony in Battery Park. For many, it was both a time of grief and of healing. *The New York Times* reported, "Jane Pollicino did not quite know what she would write when she picked up a marker yesterday morning and set it against a steel beam, painted white, that is to become one of the supporting columns at the base of Freedom Tower. For several hours Sunday morning on a lot in Battery Park City, relatives of victims of the 9/11 attack, as well as Gov. George E. Pataki, wrote personal messages and pasted photographs on a white-painted steel beam, more than 30 feet long, that will become a support column for Freedom Tower next year. In blue permanent ink, Mrs. Pollicino poured out a message to her husband, Steve, a bond trader who died in the north tower of the World Trade Center on Sept. 11, 2001. 'The circumstances of your death have allowed me to know you in ways I couldn't have imagined,' she wrote. 'I thank you for having been a part of your life and I thank God for our children.' She added, 'Until we meet again, 'you will be my music' ' — a reference to the Sinatra song that was played at their wedding in 1978. Scores of relatives signed their names, wrote messages and taped photographs on the beam, more than 30 feet long, which was available to be signed for five hours yesterday in a vacant lot in Battery Park City. Gov. George E. Pataki, who leaves office at the end of the month, wrote on the beam, as did Daniel Libeskind, the architect overseeing the master plan for the ground zero site. 'This beam is not only supporting a physical building, it's supporting the spirit of America,' Mr. Libeskind said."

Two days later, on December 19, the beam was welded into place, marking the beginning of actual construction. From that point on, work moved quickly, with most of the foundation work completed by New Year's Eve.

Even at this point, some people took offense at the way in which the building was shaping up. Architecture critic Nicolai Ouroussoff wrote in the March 4, 2007 edition of the *New York Times*, "Like their 13th- to 15th-century counterparts, contemporary architects are being enlisted to create not only major civic landmarks but lines of civic defense, with aesthetically pleasing features like elegantly sculpted barriers around public plazas or decorative cladding for bulky protective concrete walls. This vision may seem closer in spirit to da Vinci's drawings of angular fortifications or Michelangelo's designs for organically shaped bastions than to a post-cold-war-era of high-tech surveillance. ... The most chilling example of the new medievalism is New York's Freedom Tower, which was once touted as a symbol of enlightenment. Designed by David Childs of Skidmore, Owings & Merrill, it rests on a 20-story, windowless fortified concrete base decorated in prismatic glass panels in a grotesque attempt to disguise its underlying paranoia. And the brooding, obelisk-like form above is more of an expression of

American hubris than of freedom. ... The notion that we can design our way out of these problems should give us pause, however. Our streets may be prettier, but the prettiness is camouflage for the budding reality of a society ruled by fear."

   2008 saw the beginning of construction in earnest, as the concrete pillar that would form the center of the building was poured. By mid-March, the work had reached ground level and New Yorkers could finally see the progress for themselves. By the end of the first year, there was both steel and concrete showing about ground level, and progress continued in 2009 as huge steel columns were installed and floors began to take shape.

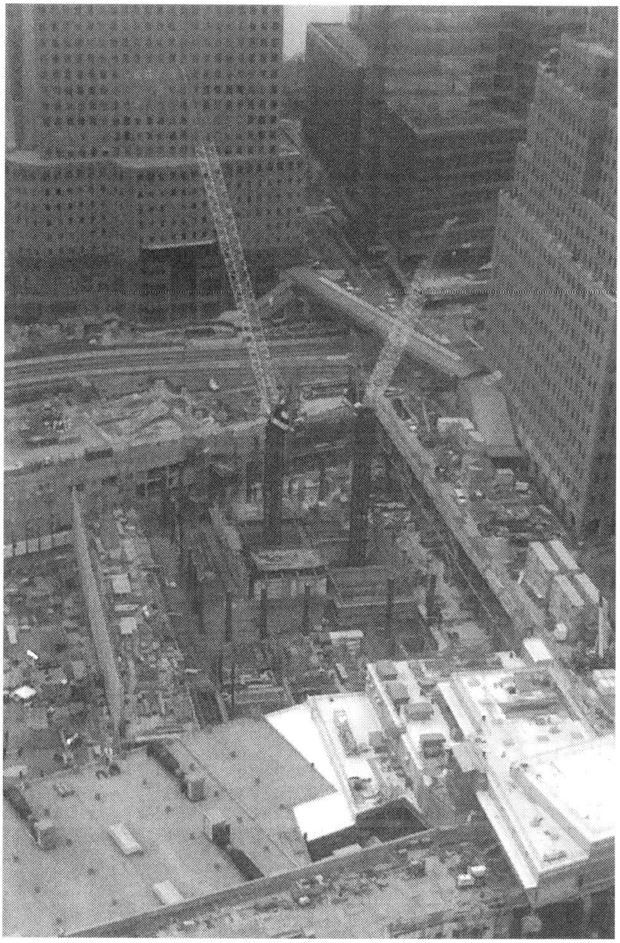

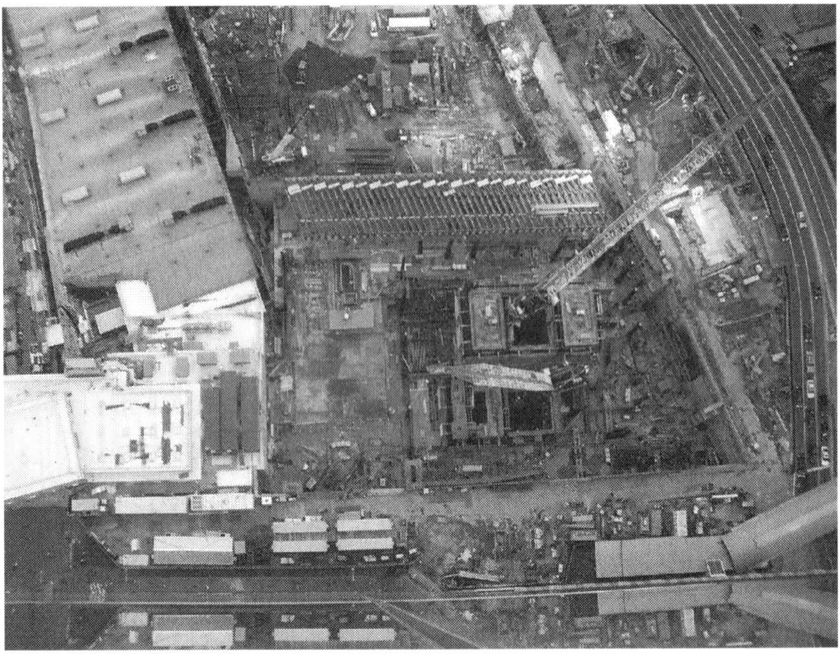

Pictures of the construction in 2008

At the same time, it seemed it would be impossible for a structure created out of the rubble of the most heinous act of the 21st century to ever escape the controversy that shaped it. More trouble emerged in 2009 when the Port Authority announced that they would no longer be calling the building "Freedom Tower." Defending this decision, spokesman Stephen Sigmund explained, "We've referred to the primary building planned for the site as One World Trade Center -- its legal name and street address -- for almost two years now, as well as using the name the Freedom Tower. Many will always refer to it as the Freedom Tower, but as the building moves out of the planning stage and into full construction and leasing, we believe that going forward it is most practical to market the building as One World Trade Center. The fact is, more than $3 billion of public money is invested in that building, and, as a public agency, we have the responsibility to make sure it is completed and that we utilize the best strategy to make certain it is fully occupied."

Then Mayor of New York Michael Bloomberg supported the decision, adding, "It's up to the

Port Authority. I have no idea what the commercial aspects are, and we can say, 'Oh, we shouldn't worry about that,' but of course you have to, particularly now. I would like to see it stay the Freedom Tower, but it's their building, and they don't need me dumping on it. If they could rent the whole thing by changing the name, I guess they're going to do that, and they probably, from a responsible point of view, should. From a patriotic point of view, is it going to make any difference? …one of the things is, we call things what we want to call them. So, Avenue of the Americas is a good example, for it's Sixth Avenue to most people. Very few people use Avenue of the Americas. If they name this One World Trade Center, people will still call it the Freedom Tower."

Bloomburg's predecessor, Rudy Giuliani, disagreed, emphatically stating, "I think it's a mistake, a big mistake. It should have a patriotic name. It's the scene of the worst attack in the history of America. It's a symbol of what happened when terrorists tried to defeat us. It's a symbol of the bravery of the police officers, the firefighters – the rescue workers that stood up immediately and didn't cave in to that type of pressure. One World Trade Center is the address, not the name of the building. As to it being more marketable – it wasn't terribly marketable as One World Trade Center. It was never a successful building."

While all this was going on, the tower continued to grow, and by April 2010, its upper levels were beginning to take on their octagonal shape. The pace picked up, as a new floor was added each week during that summer. However, the biggest surprise came not from above the ground but from below it when, on July 13, workers found the hull of an 18th century ship buried deep beneath the ground in an area being excavated for the building's Vehicle Security Center. The *Los Angeles Times* reported, "Workers excavating at the World Trade Center site have unearthed the 32-foot-long hull of a ship probably buried in the 18th century. The vessel probably was used along with other debris to fill in land to extend lower Manhattan into the Hudson River, archeologists said. Archeologists Molly McDonald and A. Michael Pappalardo were at the site of the Sept. 11, 2001, attacks on Tuesday morning when workers uncovered the artifacts. 'We noticed curved timbers that a backhoe brought up,' McDonald said Wednesday. 'We quickly found the rib of a vessel and continued to clear it away and expose the hull over the last two days.' The two archeologists work for AKRF, a firm hired to document artifacts discovered at the site. They called Tuesday's find significant but said more study was needed to determine the age of the ship. 'We're going to send timber samples to a laboratory to do endocrinology that will help us to get a sense of when the boat was constructed,' said McDonald, who added that a boat specialist was going to the site Thursday to take a look at the ship. The workers and archeologists also found a 100-pound anchor in the same area on Wednesday, but they're not sure if it belongs to the ship. The archeologists are racing to record and analyze the vessel before the delicate wood, now exposed to air, begins to deteriorate. 'I kept thinking of how closely it came to being destroyed,' Pappalardo said."

The construction site in 2009, by Ronnie Liew

Chapter 15: Completion

"The steel skeleton atop One World Trade Center is complete, reaching 105 stories – with the building's glass 'skin' and a spire soon to follow. ... The 'presidential' beam was signed by President Barack Obama when he visited the site on June 14. Also signing the symbolic white beam were Gov. Chris Christie, New York Gov. Andrew Cuomo, New York City Mayor Michael Bloomberg and site construction workers. One World Trade Center reclaimed its title as the tallest building in New York on April 30, when a 26-foot-high beam was hoisted and bolted into place, making the tower 1,271 feet high – not counting a 308-foot broadcast antenna that will top the building. The next major work will be installation of the base for the spire and antenna mast, [Bill] Baroni said. That will bring the building's height to 1,776 feet. That spire will be hoisted to the top of the trade center in pieces after the concrete base is installed, he said. ... As the tower has risen, progress on One World Trade Center has been visible from miles away in New York and New Jersey. Other parts of the site, including the transportation hub connecting PATH trains to ferries and 10 New York City subway lines, are becoming recognizable, Baroni said. ... Completion of One World Trade Center is scheduled for the fourth quarter of 2013 or the first quarter of 2014, officials said." - Larry Higgs, *Ashbury Park Press,* August 30, 2012

By the end of 2010, the builders had installed the first stainless steel and glass panels on the building, which was now more than 50 stories tall. Writing on November 17 for the *Tribeca Tribune*, Matt Dunning observed, "On Sunday, Nov. 13, crews installed the first pieces of its shiny steel-and-glass façade, on three corners and in the center of the 20th floor's eastern wall. The windows are the first to be installed anywhere on the site since the rebuilding began. 'This is another tangible sign of progress that people who walk past the site can see as we work to get this tower completed in 2013,' said Steven Coleman, spokesman for the Port Authority, the building's developer. ... 'Once they get rolling, they'll be able to install glass panels at a rate of one floor per week,' Coleman said. One at a time, each steel and glass panel is wheeled to the tower's outer edge with a hand-operated forklift, lowered into place and then bolted tight to the tower's frame. Glass is added in once the steel panel is secure. When the 1,776-foot tower is complete, crews will have placed more than 12,000 flat panels and 700 corner pieces. It will take approximately 160 panels to wrap one of the larger, lower floors in the tower, while the upper floors will need around 100 panels. Installation of the 13-foot-high panels began on the 20th floor, Coleman said, because the Port Authority will need open access to the tower's base, containing the mechanical equipment, for several more months. 'There is a lot of equipment that still needs to be loaded onto the mechanical floors in the [base], so the glass wall must come in later,' Coleman said. 'Additionally, with all the activity at the base of the building now, we scheduled the wall later to minimize damage.'"

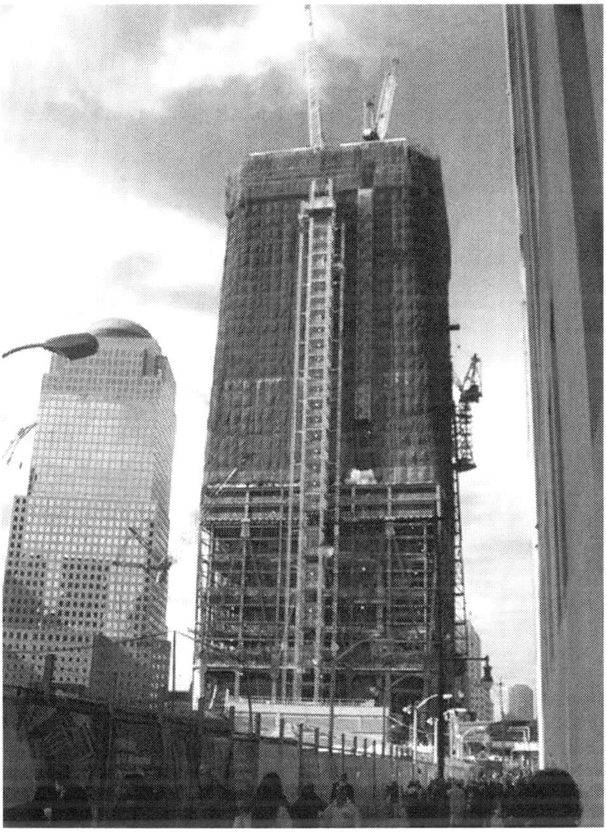

Pictures of the Freedom Tower in 2010

    Progress continued at a steady pace throughout 2011 but slowed in 2012, as workers were hampered by unusually high winds and ice. Because of these and other concerns, it took workers two months to complete their work on the 92nd floor. Progress then picked up again with better weather, and on June 21, 2012, the roof was placed on the top story of the building. Two months later, a special beam signed by President Barack Obama and others was put in place. Bill Baroni, Port Authority of New York and New Jersey deputy executive director, announced happily, "We have topped out at 105 stories. We put the president's beam in two weeks ago and topped out the steel — you can literally stand on the roof The big thing you can see is the glass will go in faster. ... You can see it taking that shape that our (conceptual) pictures show." This marked a critical moment in the building's completion, according to James Hughes, a professor at Rutgers University, who added, "About one year ago when One World Trade Center started to be visible (in the skyline), it was thrilling to see how the Goldman Sachs tower (in Jersey City) played off it. It's a signature event — it can only help with the marketability of lower Manhattan. We'll see how it plays out. ... The real driving force is Conde Nast moving from 42nd Street to the World Trade Center. Their decision to locate on 42nd Street transformed it from a frontier to a hot place to bet. (One WTC) will still be subject to cyclical (economic) forces. Market forces are still in play in filling the rest of the building. ... Once the transportation center opens, they may be the key to transforming it into a spectacular space. You're bringing in subway lines that were previously disjointed; you'll have the soaring PATH hall and connections to everything underground that many can't imagine. It will make it (the site) more attractive."

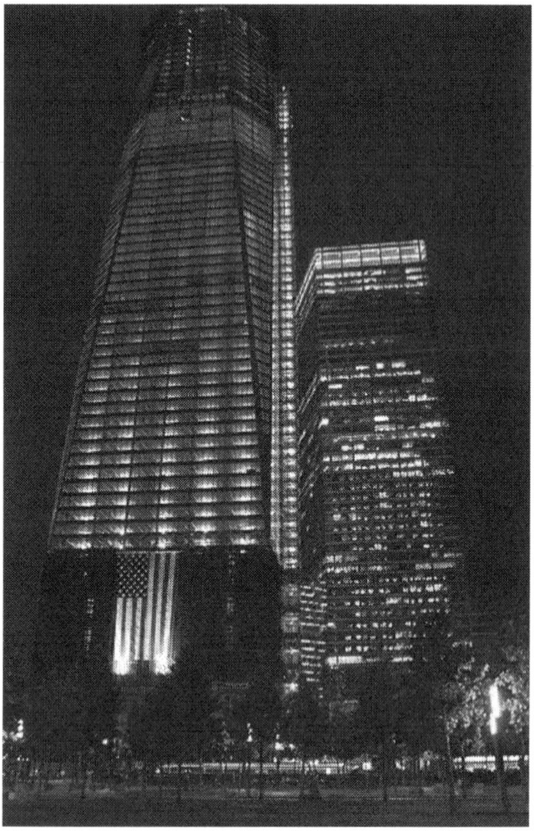

Pictures of the Freedom Tower in 2011, by David Shankebone

The Freedom Tower just months before completion, by Benjamin Powell

    Meanwhile, work was completed on the 408 foot spire that would make One World Trade Center the tallest building in the United States. On May 2, 2013, the *New York Times* reported, "Looking a bit like a rocket taking flight, the spire of 1 World Trade Center was hoisted aloft on Thursday and set on a temporary platform atop the nearly completed building. When it is bolted into place at a later date, the spire will bring the building to a height of 1,776 feet." Ironically, this symbol of American triumph had been constructed in Canada in 16 separate sections before being shipped to the United States for installation. The final pieces were put in place on May 10, by the end of the year, One World Trade Center was ready to open. It had cost nearly $4 billion to complete, making it the most expensive building ever completed. A quarter of its cost came from Silverstein, and the insurance money he received following 9/11. Another billion came from the Port Authority and a quarter-billion from the State of New York. The rest of the cost was raised elsewhere.

Writing for ABC News, Josh Margolin announced on November 3, 2014, "It's finally done. Thirteen years after the Twin Towers were destroyed on Sept. 11, 2001, the new centerpiece skyscraper at the World Trade Center opens this morning. The path to this day was anything but easy or clear. Battles began almost as soon as the debris was hauled away in 2002 and, since then, there have been fights over cost, design, security and even the structure's name. But still, the tower – a technological marvel sitting on piles driven more than 100 feet below the Hudson River – rose steadily out of the northwest corner of the WTC site. ... In so many ways, this day marks the final piece of the rebirth and renewal of a Lower Manhattan devastated when two hijacked jets slammed into the Twin Towers that bright morning. On Sept. 11, 2011, the 9/11 Memorial opened. Six months ago, the 9/11 Museum opened. Both were built to commemorate what was lost. One World Trade is a monument to the future."

Steve Plate, the man who oversaw the construction, added, "It's a fantastic milestone. I was there that fateful day. And to see from where we started to where we are today, it's truly a miracle. It truly is the eighth wonder of the world. And the building itself is truly iconic. ... I'm an engineer and I can add numbers and tell you 'tallest, strongest' and all this stuff. But at the end of the day, it's the most beautiful building in the most beautiful city in the most beautiful region in the world."

Dave Checkets, whose company Legends was in charge of the observatory on the top of the new building, emotionally noted, "There's so many people who have done so much to bring it where it is. I give them all a lot of credit for staying with the fight because the finished product is going to be something inspirational to people and comforting. It's a brute fact. We did come back. We brought it back; we built it even higher than it was before."

One World Trade Center as seen from its base, by John D. Morris

Chapter 16: Consummation

"More than 13 years after a terrorist attack destroyed the Twin Towers — soaring symbols of New York City's might, financially and structurally — the first employees of the first tenant in the building erected to take their place arrived on Monday for their first workday. "The building is open for business," said Jordan Barowitz, an official of the Durst Organization, which developed the building, 1 World Trade Center, with the Port Authority of New York and New Jersey. "It's a beautiful building, it's a historic building, but it's an office building and it's open for business." At 1,776 feet in height, the building is steps from where the north tower stood until Sept. 11, 2001. But where that sunny morning held a still-summery promise until the first jetliner lacerated 1 World Trade Center and smoke filled the jewel-blue sky, Monday was chilly and windy as employees of the magazine publisher Condé Nast arrived. They walked under the lobby's high ceilings, adorned in white marble from the same quarry as the old towers — one of the many details that will remind them that their new workplace has an unavoidable connection to that day, and to the pledges of renewal made by elected officials and ordinary citizens alike. In the lobby of the new building. The lobby is adorned with white marble from the same quarry that produced the marble in the old twin towers." - James Barron, writing for *The New York Times* on November 3, 2014

Mark Wyman's picture of the Freedom Tower's entrance

Those walking into the new World Trade Center when it opened saw a place that was a far cry from Libeskind's original design, but then again very few large structures end up looking exactly like they were intended to be. It was in many ways more symmetrical and consistent with the other buildings around it. Its spire not only made it the tallest building in the Western Hemisphere but also tied it in to other such notable structures as the Empire State Building and the Chrysler Building. Perhaps the building's most distinct feature is its shape, which begins to change at the 20th floor from a perfect square to an octagon, only to return again to a square shape at the top. Childs praised this shape, saying, "Tapered buildings, like the John Hancock Tower in Chicago, are stronger than straight up-and-down rectangles. Really, there is an extremely long list of safety innovations that I could cite about the Tower. But in the end, I think the most important thing for the public to know about this building is that its form is inherently extremely strong." Likewise, the Port Authority boasted, "The ultra-modern design of One World Trade Center is an innovative mix of architecture, safety and sustainability. The building's simplicity and clarity of form are timeless, extending the long tradition of American ingenuity in high-rise construction. One World Trade Center will be a new visual landmark for New York and the United States. Its structure is designed around a strong, redundant steel frame, consisting of beams and columns. Paired with a concrete-core shear wall, the redundant steel frame lends substantial rigidity and redundancy to the overall building structure while providing column-free interior spans for maximum flexibility. The building incorporates highly advanced state-of-the-art life-safety systems that exceed the requirements of the New York City Building Code and that will lead the way in developing new innovative technology for high-rise building standards. Through unprecedented collaborations with technology and energy leaders throughout the world, One World Trade Center's design team used the latest methods to maximize efficiency, minimize waste and pollution, conserve water, improve air quality and reduce the impacts of the development. Taking advantage of the next generation of innovative energy sources, as well as off-site renewable wind and hydro power, One World Trade Center is slated to be both safe and environmentally friendly."

Of course, having a beautiful building was useless without people working in it, and the Port Authority promised that the new World Trade Center was as accessible as it was beautiful: "Workers commuting to One World Trade Center will enjoy unprecedented access to mass transit service. Dazzling new climate-controlled corridors will connect One World Trade Center to the WTC Transportation Hub and the new PATH terminal, 11 NYC Transit subway lines and the new Fulton Street Transit Center, the World Financial Center and ferry terminal, underground parking and world-class shopping and dining. One World Trade Center's location in Lower Manhattan positions it in close proximity to amenities at the World Financial Center, Battery Park City and the new West Side Promenade, as well as offers easy access to Tribeca, South Street Seaport and Wall Street. Neighborhood amenities include world-class shopping and a riverfront walkway in a mixed-use community that is active 24/7."

Naturally, for most people, moving into One World Trade was much different than moving into any other office building. For one thing, there was the ongoing awareness that they were moving into a popular terrorist target. The feeling was so strong that comedian Chris Rock joked on *Saturday Night Live*, "They should change the name from the Freedom Tower to the 'Never Going in There Tower,' because I'm never going in there. There is no circumstance that will ever get me in that building." At the same time, others felt a certain defiance, such as was expressed by Vijay Ramcharitar, a 25 year old Conde Nast employee who admitted, "I can understand the fear behind it. ... If you live in fear, you can't get anything done in your life."

Indeed, others realized that the building was probably safer than most because of the way in which it was constructed, and the care that those involved in its security would take. These security measures were already well in place when the first employees arrived. Barron noted, "Condé Nast's chief executive, Charles H. Townsend, pulled up to the south entrance in a Mercedes-Benz limousine as his subordinates walked in. If they had arrived in cars with drivers, they could not have turned onto Vesey Street — retractable metal bollards have been installed in the pavement to block access. They were up on Monday morning, and police officers had been posted around the building. And the employees who entered the Vesey Street door flashed an identification pass; they flashed it again when they reached the turnstiles that control access to the elevators. Austin D. Parker, who works for an audiovisual installation company hired by Condé Nast, said employees had been steeped in security protocols and procedures. He said he had been given instruction in escape routes. ... For many people in Lower Manhattan, Monday was the day to acknowledge the reknitting of the trade center site into the fabric of the city. At the sidewalk level, the area immediately around it had been off limits for so long that 1 World Trade remained somewhat remote, even as thousands of workers rushed by on their way to offices in the complex across nearby West Street that was known on Sept. 11 as the World Financial Center. (It is now called Brookfield Place.)"

It would still be awhile before someone wishing to go to the building's three story observation deck could take an elevator past 18 underground floors and 86 above ground floors, almost all of the latter devoted to office space. In the meanwhile, visitors would have to make do with the 64th floor to see the sky lobby.

Ironically, the underground portion of the building may be even more interesting than the view, as one writer for *Scribol* magazine noted: "The construction process itself had to take into consideration the maze of complex infrastructure under the One World Trade Center, such as train tracks, underground pedestrian tunnels, power lines and the subway. A portion of the site was even underwater…Rebuilding on the site of the Twin Towers attacks also carries a lot of emotional and symbolic weight, and the structure contains small but significant tributes to freedom and the building that came before it. One World Trade Center's architectural height of 1,776 feet (541 meters) was designed as a reference to the year that the United States Declaration of Independence was signed, while the window-washing tracks will be located in the 110th floor, as a reminder of the 110 stories of the former World Trade Center buildings. Its footprint is also 200 feet (61 meters) square, almost the same as the footprint of the old towers. Perhaps the most poignant symbol of all, though, stands outside of the tower. It's a bronze monument picturing a soldier on a horse, with a piece of steel from the original World Trade Center embedded in its base. It's titled 'America's Response Monument', is a tribute to US military forces who operated during the war in Afghanistan and is emblazoned at its base with the Latin phrase 'de opresso liber', meaning 'to free the oppressed'. The soldier himself is positioned to face One World Trade Center, as if keeping a constant watch over it, protecting it and keeping it safe."

America's Response Monument, by Douwe Blumberg

Kai Brinker's picture of the observatory deck

Chapter 17: Consequence

"Justin Casquejo, 16, and his pals, who are part of a stunt-loving group of youth who call themselves 'Team Destiny,' had probed the security of the 1,776-foot-tall skyscraper on three occasions in hopes of slipping inside, but never managed to elude the network of watchmen.... But in the end, Casquejo pulled it off on his own in the pre-dawn hours of Sunday. ... On Sunday morning Casquejo left his family's home and ventured to lower Manhattan, approaching 1 World Trade Center shortly after 4 a.m. The slender teen slipped through a small hole — measuring 12 inches by 12 inches — in the construction fence surrounding the site. He then climbed up scaffolding encasing the tower and did his best Spiderman impersonation until he found an entry point on the sixth floor. ... It was then he got his first break. An elevator operator somehow did not get suspicious at the sight of the adolescent trespasser and allowed him to hitch a ride up to the 88th floor — never bothering to check whether Casquejo had a security pass, officials said. From there Casquejo hoofed it up to the 104th floor, where he ran into his second break — a security guard was sound asleep. He walked right by the man and made his way onto the roof. 'I went to the rooftop and climbed the ladder all the way to the antenna,' Casquejo admitted, according to court documents. A Port Authority police officer ultimately grabbed

Casquejo on the 104th floor at 6 a.m. — two hours after he breached the gates, officials said." - Joseph Stepansky and Thomas Tracy, "Daredevil teen sneaked into 1 World Trade Center, spent two hours at base of antenna taking pictures," *New York Daily News*

The completed One World Trade Center, courtesy of Joe Mabel

There is a certain set of consequences that go along with being one of the most famous buildings in the world. The most obvious, especially given the past, is that such a structure is a target for modern day terrorists. Much like the German Luftwaffe targeted the cathedrals of London during the blitz, America's enemies have repeatedly targeted its "cathedrals of capitalism," striking at the essence of the country.

Another consequence is that many people will look for a chance to make a name for themselves by using the building. In September 2013, Jim Brady, Marko Markovich and Andrew Rossig base jumped off the top of the building. On another occasion in March 2014, 16 year old Justin Casquejo of New Jersey broke into the site and made his way past guards all the way to the top of the building, climbing the spire and taking pictures. Had he done the same to any other large office building, the incident might have gone unnoticed, but because it was the Freedom Tower, the story made both national and inter-national news.

Ultimately, the main consequence of completing One World Trade Center was that it would have to be occupied. This proved to be something of a challenge during the financial downturn that was plaguing the country at the time it opened. However, in addition to the already mentioned occupation by Conde Nast, the Port Authority was also able to lease space on a long term basis to Vantone Industiral, a Beijing-based company that leased several floors to use for both cultural and business purposes.

Eventually, a surprising number of companies leasing space in the rebuilt One World Trade Center came not from Wall Street but from the West Coast. Bloomburg News reported in January 2015, "When lower Manhattan's new World Trade Center was conceived a decade ago, nobody had in mind a Silicon Valley in the sky. Financial companies, which dominated the original twin towers, are scarce among tenants who have committed to space at the complex's glass-and-steel skyscrapers. Instead, the majority of deals done since magazine publisher Conde Nast agreed to anchor 1 World Trade Center in 2011 have come from technology, media and advertising. 'People were expecting financial companies to be a substantial portion of the leased space' in the new towers, said Christopher Jones, vice president of research at New York's Regional Plan Association. 'I don't think many people would have thought that it would be virtually nothing.' ... The banking and insurance industries, which occupied almost 80% of the old World Trade Center's leased space, make up 1.3% of current tenants.... Media, advertising, computer-technology and communications companies have taken almost 33% of the space rented so far, compared with only about 3% at the old World Trade Center.... About 40% is from government tenants that agreed to lease space in the middle of the last decade to help jumpstart construction of the towers. The remainder came from business services, real estate and other fields. For High 5 Games, a developer of casino and social media games, 1 World Trade Center was 'complementary to Silicon Valley on the West Coast,' said Patrick Benson, vice president of marketing. The firm, currently based at 770 Broadway in the East Village, took 87,663 square feet on floors 58 and 59. 'It provided everything that we needed,' including state-of-the-art technology, a 'blank slate' of column-free offices, and room for expansion, Mr. Benson said."

As of early 2015, only a bit over 60% of the space in the tower was rented out. Still, owners remained optimistic. The article continued, "The presence of xAd, High 5 and MediaMath shows the Trade Center can lure technology and other creative companies away from such neighborhoods as Chelsea, Soho and the Flatiron District. Demand in those areas, part of a district known as midtown south, has pushed office vacancies to the lowest in the U.S. 'Attracting some of the tech users this year was something we thought might have taken a little longer to develop,' Tara Stacom, the Cushman and Wakefield Inc. broker working with Durst to fill 1 World Trade Center, said in an interview last month. 'They realized the value of new construction was something they weren't getting in midtown south.' XAd and High 5 Games are paying about $55 to $60 a square foot at 1 World Trade, minus any incentives such as government subsidies and free-rent periods, according to data from research firm Compstak. That's more than the average effective rent of $44 a square foot for the best-quality space in lower Manhattan. ... One World Trade Center was at the top of the list when Servcorp Ltd. shopped for a fourth New York location, said Chief Operating Officer Marcus Moufarrige. The Sydney-based firm provides temporary high-end offices to global companies, targeting the most famous and opulent properties in the markets it serves, such as London's 'Cheesegrater.' 'We've been working on this deal for three years,' said Mr. Moufarrige, whose company rented about 35,000 square feet at 1 World Trade, the entire 85th floor. 'It's going to be the most iconic building in the world. There was no hesitation in us wanting to be there.'"

A final consequence of completing and opening any building is coping with graffiti. However, the words scrawled in various places on One World Trade Center were different from those elsewhere for several reasons. For one thing, most of what was written was done to the interior of the building as it was being constructed. Many workers wrote defiant slogans such as "Freedom Forever. WTC 9/11," "Change is from within" and "God Bless the workers & inhabitants of this bldg." Another thing that makes One World Trade Center's graffiti "problem" different is that most people want to preserve rather than erase the words that ironworker Kevin Murphy called "things from the heart." He explained, "This is not just any construction site, this is a special place for these guys. Everyone here wants to be here, they want to put this building up. They're part of the redemption."

According to a 2013 article from the *Huffington Post*, "In the rooftop iron scaffolding for the spire, 105 floors up, a beam pays homage to Lillian Frederick, a 46-year-old administrative assistant who died on the 105th floor of the south tower, pierced by a terrorist-hijacked airliner. A popular Spanish phrase is penned next to two names on one concrete pillar: 'Te Amo Tres Metros Sobre el Cielo,' meaning, 'I love you three steps above heaven.' Some beams are almost completely covered in a spaghetti-like jumble of doodled hearts and flowers, loopy cursives and blaring capitals. Many want to simply mark their presence: 'Henry Wynn/Plumbers Local (hash)1/Sheepshead Bay/Never Forget!' Families of victims invited to go up left names and comments too, as did firefighters and police officers who were first responders. 'R.I.P. Fanny Espinoza, 9-11-01' reads a typical remembrance signed by several family members of a Cantor-Fitzgerald employee. Former Homeland Security Secretary Michael Chertoff wrote: 'With you in spirit – those who perished, those who fought, those who build.' Time and daily routines have softened the communal grief as the workers carry on, trading jokes and gruff male banter. Some ends up in whimsical graffiti marking World Cup soccer matches, New York Giants Super Bowl victories and other less-weighty matters that have gone on since construction began six years ago. One crudely drawn map of the neighborhood down below shows the location of a popular strip club. People on the ground below will never see the spontaneous private thoughts high in the Manhattan sky. The graffiti will disappear as the raw basic structure is covered with drywall, ceiling panels and paint for tenants moving into the 3 million square feet of office space by 2014. Knowing this, workers and visitors often take photographs of special bits of graffiti, so the words will live on."

View from the September 11 Memorial.

Online Resources

Other books about New York City by Charles River Editors

Other books about the World Trade Center on Amazon

Bibliography

Darton, Eric (1999). *Divided We Stand: A Biography of New York's World Trade Center.* Basic Books.

Gillespie, Angus K. (1999). *Twin Towers: The Life of New York City's World Trade Center.* Rutgers University Press.

Reeve, Simon (1999). *The New Jackals: Ramzi Yousef, Osama bin Laden and the Future of Terrorism.* Northeastern University Press.

Ruchelman, Leonard I. (1977). *The World Trade Center: Politics and Policies of Skyscraper Development.* Syracuse University Press.

Printed in Poland
by Amazon Fulfillment
Poland Sp. z o.o., Wrocław